The Path to
Well-Being

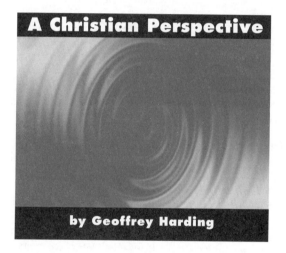

A Christian Perspective

by Geoffrey Harding

John Hunt
Publishing Limited

Copyright © 2003 John Hunt Publishing Ltd
46A West Street, Alresford, Hants SO24 9AU, U.K.
Tel: +44 (0) 1962 736880 Fax: +44 (0) 1962 736881
E-mail: office@johnhunt-publishing.com
www.johnhunt-publishing.com

Text: © 2003 The Relaxation Society

Designed by Nautilus Design

ISBN 1 84298-101-3

A CIP catalogue record for this book is available from the British
Library.

The Relaxation Society is a Registered Charity No. 233123
Cassette tapes are available from the Relaxation Society.
For details contact:
The Secretary
The Relaxation Society
84 Herbert Gardens
Willesden, London NW10 3BU

Printed in the U.K. by Ashford Colour Press

Opposite page: St Mary Woolnoth

The Path to Well-Being

A Christian Perspective

by Geoffrey Harding,
the author of
Lying Down in Church
and
Founder of the Relaxation Society

Foreword by The Rt Rev Dr David Jenkins

CONTENTS

Editor's Note

At one time I was particularly affected by someone else's problem, which I could do nothing to alleviate. I was advised to 'let go and let God'.

I thought this demanded a mental and spiritual change on my part. It was only later, by pure chance, I found myself at St Mary Woolnoth, a church at the end of Lombard Street, London being told *how* to let go; that I am basically an animal but misuse my animal defence mechanisms. Before I can undo my mental stress I must accept the basic truth of "First the Physical" (the motto of the Relaxation Society) to become aware of and then undo needless physical tension. Only then could the mental and spiritual change start to happen.

Lying on the floor of the church I was helped into a state of relaxation, and listened and absorbed such as: -

'God has given a little part of himself to each one of us - more than we shall ever need. He yearns only that we use it.'

'God is everywhere; there is nowhere that God is not'.

'It is not so important that you believe in God; the important thing is God believes in you!'

'A wish is a prayer.'

I found relaxation was not an end in itself, (enjoyable as it is), but the beginning of a much more complete and satisfying life, even if that, at times, is only enjoying the next in-breath and the following out-breath.

Apart from his book, *Lying Down In Church*, the writings of Geoffrey Harding have previously only been published as pamphlets for the Relaxation Society. This book is published to make them more suitably available for the public at large.

The Society was formed in the early 1960s to further Geoffrey's belief that being relaxed is the first essential condition to well-being and self-fulfilment. Successful actors and athletes are particularly aware of this from an early stage in their careers. For myself, I remember my school reports: 'Tries hard, could do better' or something to that effect. If only someone had written: 'Tries too hard, would do better if he relaxed!' I had no idea at the time that I was so intense, and it was only many years later, as I lay on the floor of St Mary Woolnoth, that I learnt what the word 'relax' really meant.

My thanks go to David Jenkins for his Foreword, to Denis Duncan for his encouragement, to Richard Hudson for his help in amalgamating some pamphlets which had a common theme, and to Maurice Kidd for his advice and proof reading, also to Gerald Whiting for much guidance and help as I familiarised myself in operating a PC and to Malcolm Pusey for the finishing touches to my typing.

Geoff Hayden, Dartford, August 2001

Foreword by the Rt Revd Dr David Jenkins

I first met Geoffrey Harding in the 1960s when he was working heroically to widen the outlook of the Churches' Council for Healing. He transformed it from a rather sectarian collection of faith healers into a Churches' Council for Health and Healing equipped to take a central part in pursuing the broader issues of medicine, psychology and pastoral practice with which he was, in his own well-informed and learned way, concerned. He involved me as Chairman of the Council in this process and through the 1960s and 70s we had many deep discussions in which I was both impressed and helped by his wide reading, clear perception and depth of theological insight.

Geoffrey was an up-to-date version of an old fashioned style of Anglican clergyman. Before he took his theology degree, he read Greats (Greek and Latin language and literature followed by ancient history, classical philosophy and modern logic). This gave him a wide interest in traditional thought about being human. He combined that interest with a fine critical mind. Throughout his ministry he combined traditional thought with modern developments in medicine and psychology in his approach to working out our understanding of human nature, human development and human relationships.

So he was old-fashioned in his traditional scholarly approach to both the pastoral work and the missionary work of the Church and the Ministry. He was old-fashioned, too, in his determination to pursue his very individual way of working out how to relate developments in medicine and psychology with pastoral practice. He was rigorous in his thinking and through discussions with practitioners in medicine and psychology developed a careful and theologically informed approach to the humane practice of medicine and developments in both medical and pastoral care.

He was old-fashioned too in that he combined all this with a down-to-earth ministry and involvement in the daily life of the people among whom he served. As a chaplain in the RAF during the War of 1939–1945 he was awarded an MC for his bravery in the D-Day landings on Omaha Beach. Back in parish life he majored on contacts between doctors and clergy and on the dynamic and practical connections between theological understanding, medical practice and psychological problems. This led him into a very deep concern for promoting serious and sustained study, both theoretical and practical, between doctors, clergy and interested laity, in the practices of healthcare.

Thus Geoffrey was an old-fashioned Anglican clergyman in the tradition of those who, at one time, gained a reputation for combining learning with down-to-earth pastoral and parochial practice by their determination to follow an idiosyncratic approach of their own.

I do not think Geoffrey's talents were ever harnessed in the wider affairs of the Church as the relevance of his combination of interests merited. Nonetheless, behind the scenes, and in his own inimitable and very determined way, he was quietly influential. He was of great use in opening up, exploring and developing working relationships in the inter-locking fields of medical practice, psychological developments and practical pastoralia – all related to a search for an enlarged understanding of what it is to be human. At first glance he seemed a rather lonely man who pursued a somewhat eccentric ministry. In fact he was focusing on some fundamentally central pastoral and theological issues. He was deeply and practically concerned to combine modern developments in medicine and psychology with basic theological and pastoral traditions of Christian faith. I think, on reflection, that his greatest ministry and service was to numerous individuals (myself included) from a variety of professions, stages of faith and human bewilderment. I remember him, therefore, above all as a remarkably sensitive priest.

After all the stresses and strains which he had to endure – organisational, theological and the pressure of limitations of money and resources – it seemed very right and proper that he should have been appointed to serve as the priest-in-charge of St Mary Woolnoth, Lombard Street, in the City of London. There he developed a centre for tackling stress and in particular the work of the Relaxation Society. This was personal pastoral work which helped very many individuals. It is a good thing therefore that colleagues in the Relaxation Society should have banded together to produce these occasional papers of his. When quietly considered they convey the very particular nature of his approach and insights. Both wide-ranging and yet drawn together by Geoffrey's clear, practical and personal focus, they provide material which should help many in their own need for quietness and reflection, relaxation and refocusing. Given the increasing busy-ness and stress of the lives of so many, we have here an important collection of quiet but forceful Tracts for the Times.

CHAPTER ONE

Stress

Disease or Dis-ease

What is stress?

Stress is the built-in alarm mechanism of the whole personality in the face of danger. Consider what happens when I find myself alone with an angry bull in a large empty field: I feel a high degree of alarm and take to my heels and run, or scramble up the nearest tree. Or if I am caught on the main road with an enormous truck coming straight at me, I throw myself at the pavement in a wild leap.

This is the normal working of the alarm reaction (which may well have saved my life before now). Its sole purpose is to get me out of harm's way.

What actually happens? Directly I see (or hear) danger the great nerve centres at the base of the brain take over. Every resource in body and mind is immediately mobilised to get me out of danger. The muscles in my arms and legs and trunk tense like springs; I move faster than I would have thought possible. To support this terrific outburst of energy I need supplies of oxygen and sugar. (Sugar is the raw material of physical energy and oxygen burns it up.) So my lungs take in all the oxygen they can get and my heart works overtime to distribute it all over the body. On its way the circulating blood picks up sugar from the liver, the body's reserve energy store. I am now all keyed up and bursting with energy.

This is the basic mechanism of anger and fear, which we experience through all its stages from vague apprehension or mild irritation to blind panic or uncontrolled fury. It is very clearly seen in any animal – in the cat for example, when the dog is chasing it: back arched, fur fluffed up, claws out, spitting, poised to slash the dog's nose or rush up the nearest tree. Attack and go for your enemy, or go for safety as fast as you can. That is why it is referred to as the 'fight-flight' reaction.

This is a beautiful mechanism, which serves its purpose admirably in any situation of real, physical danger. Just as pain warns me of hurt and damage in my body, so fear gives me advance warning of danger and gives me the chance of escape. Anger, which is physically very close to fear, is the extra energy I can throw into the fight if it is going against me. It is largely a matter of what I am up against. If my opponent is smaller than I am, I can afford to be angry but if he is bigger than I am, I am wise to feel frightened.

This is the normal physical reaction to danger and we could hardly live without it. The catch is that it comes on automatically in any situation in which we feel threatened. In everyday life however, real physical emergencies are few. We no longer expect to find a wild animal lurking behind the next bush. Come to that, we are not exposed, at any rate in times of peace, to most of the physical hazards that our forefathers would have taken for granted.

We no longer have to have a tooth out or a leg off without an anaesthetic, for example, and we no longer live in fear of the plague; the infant mortality rate is only a fraction of what it was in the days of Queen Anne who saw none of her children come to maturity. There are still black spots, but most of us are warmly clothed and adequately housed, and have more to eat and drink than is good for us.

So why is it that we lose 330 million working days a year through ill health; that heart trouble has gone up alarmingly in recent years, that 10 million out of 44 million adults are going to the doctor for pills of some kind to calm their nerves, and that one in four of the family doctor's patients are said to be more emotionally upset than physically ill? Where should we be without the astronomical quantities of aspirin, alcohol, caffeine and nicotine that are needed to make life tolerable for most of us?

Someone once defined dirt as 'matter in the wrong place'; one might say something similar about stress. Stress is the fight-flight reaction in the wrong place; when we are not faced by the kind of physical emergency for which it was designed, when it simply would not do to knock my opponent down, or take to my heels and run. For better or worse we have become more civilised. But it has its disadvantages, as I cannot make sensible use of the pent-up energy that the 'fight-flight' reaction provides. I cannot be angry with the boss, so do I keep my feelings under strict control or do I take it out on my wife and family when I get home? If I choose the first alternative I shall make myself ill; if the second, I shall make *them* ill. This is the basic problem of stress. In other words, stress is the alarm reaction that has become destructive rather than constructive. Because I cannot meet the situation sensibly I am driven to over-react – to say or do too much – or to under-react – to say or do too little. Either way I am not coping with the real problem.

What are the signs of stress?

When I meet a physical emergency, I cope with it and then feel a great sense of relief. The alarm reaction has done its work and my body quickly returns to normal. But when I am faced with a situation I cannot cope with, alarm persists, and the 'fight-flight' reaction goes on working. This means that all the physical processes, which are intended to rescue me from physical danger, are still doing their best for me. They now become symptoms of stress.

Thus when I detect danger, nature insists that I give my entire attention to the threat to my security: I cannot go on thinking about anything I was doing before the emergency began. So when the stress persists, one of the first symptoms is *loss of concentration*. The problem is 'on my mind' and however hard I try, I cannot throw it off. To my great annoyance (which adds to stress), it disturbs my sleep. Again, the explanation is quite simple. I am still on the alert when I go to bed; still on the watch for a possible enemy, and still very wide awake.

There are two further points that should be mentioned, as they are both part of this defensive reaction. Nature expects us to be wounded in this encounter with the enemy, and gets ready to repair the damage. So when I feel angry or frightened my skin contracts and the small blood vessels beneath the skin close up (anxiety makes me go pale). There is another effect, which is highly important. Two little glands on top of either kidney, the famous suprarenal glands, secrete adrenaline, a hormone that sustains effort. One of its functions is to make the blood coagulate and form a clot, which will plug the wound. Naturally, if I am unduly alarmed, I run the risk of blood clots and heightened blood pressure.

The other point is more general. If stress continues too long, the 'fight-flight' reaction may well give way to the opposite reaction of giving up and giving in. This too is of animal origin. It is simply that when an animal is pursued by a predator, its best chance of escape may well be to stand stock-still and freeze into the landscape. If it moves, it will be spotted: completely motionless it will escape detection. Nature again comes to the rescue by working out another ingenious mechanism to save the animal's life. The motor- nerves are stopped from sending their normal impulses to the muscles, so that the animal is rendered temporarily immobile. Anyone who has seen an animal alarmed, like the rabbit apparently hypnotised by the stoat, will have watched this mechanism at work.

This reaction, also, we have inherited: very useful in its proper place but 'paralysing' when it comes on at the wrong moment. When we are dealing with someone who cannot 'pull himself together', this is what is happening. We know what it feels like ourselves in a mild way when we feel caught or trapped in a situation we cannot get out of, or under the eye of someone who 'has it in for us'. When strain is intensified, the moment comes when we sink into a state of frozen immobility; this is the kind of panic-paralysis which the animal experiences. It is really hard to throw off. We cope somehow for a long time, but suddenly we go down into a sort of yawning abyss, in which we feel physical lowness, hopeless weariness and mental depression, in varying degrees. It can be the effect of shock, but more often it is the wear and tear of long-continued strain. It cannot be too strongly emphasised that anyone in depression needs medical help to get the nervous system working normally so that they can face the world.

Fear of ourselves

The difficulty here is that stress, as a chronic condition, started in childhood, and we have been handicapped almost from the start. To understand what has happened it will help us to distinguish between temperament, disposition and character. Temperament is what I am born with, and character is what I make of temperament: but in between them comes disposition, the early shaping of my resources before I took individual control. The infant is largely at the mercy of its surroundings and very vulnerable to others' feelings, especially to their reaction to his own. Most parents are secretly frightened of their very young children, mainly because their feelings are so total: they are totally hungry, totally frightened, totally angry, as the case may be. Given time, the primitive instinct is modified by experience: hunger grows into appetite, which is more selective, and temper grows into willpower. We usually succeed in moderating hunger, but are less successful with anger and fear, which are liable, to the end of our days, particularly in moments of stress, to show the same total infantile characteristics! In between these outbursts and attacks, we succeed in modifying them by the process we call self-control (which means using all our muscles to hold ourselves in). But at the least slackening of our will-power the unsolved problem, which we have taken over from our earliest days, is only too likely to reappear.

There are two main reasons why the problem does not work out as it should. The first is one's parent's reaction to these early feelings. Parents are apt to be dismayed at the strength of a young child's anger and feel shocked by it, which makes the child shocked and frightened himself. This disapproval is apt to remain as a permanent barrier to the working out of the problem. In later life we fail to be angry when we should be, and have no idea what use to make of anger when it is already present. There is a similar reaction to fear. Mother disguises her own fear with an excess of maternal solicitude, and in later life we detect, if we are honest, the same mixture of love and anxiety in our own make-up.

It is probably true of most of us that the fears which later seem almost impossible to control were not originally our own fears but part of the nervousness which infected us in early life. That is why they seem to go so deep and not to be 'us' at all. This disposition or whatever one should call it, makes it difficult for us to meet other people 'on the level'. There is apt to be a hidden reserve of anger which tends to make us feel superior and contemptuous, or a residue of fear which makes us feel habitually inferior or in the wrong. Either attitude is a partial attitude of distrust which stands in the way of our feeling completely at ease.

A man or woman in later life may develop great strength of character, but this will not prevent him from being undermined, from time to time, by his 'disposition'. It may occur as a functional illness, as a nervous breakdown, or as a long-standing difficulty in personal relationships in which he finds that he is always defeated by a certain type of person or situation which he can never learn to handle. Drugs and tranquillisers may help, or psychotherapy, or religion, or all of them. But in any case it is this area of the mind, underneath the will, which I have chosen to call disposition that is causing the difficulty. There is therefore, a short term and a long term answer to this problem. First-aid can be given fairly easily but the long-term answer can only be worked out gradually.

The worst effect of stress is that we are so afraid of it; the fear of fear and the shame of fear do more damage than fear itself. Once we get the idea that stress is a natural phenomenon that we are all liable to – even the strongest of us has his breaking point – the battle is half won. Anyone not affected by stress in some way or other is not human – and probably not doing his job. In this respect stress is like stage fright; a certain amount of it enables us to give a better performance. The problem is not to avoid stress but to make use of it and keep it within manageable proportions. Someone recently has invented the word 'eu-stress' to describe a challenge that we are meeting adequately. How to turn distress into eu-stress is the question we have to answer.

WHAT IS THE ANSWER?

Unconditioning the reflexes

It is possible to take the sting out of the problem by reducing the element of stress: in other words, not to regard the situation as a threat.

The first step, therefore, is to break down old habits. The obvious analogy is that of being teased at school: once we learned not to mind being teased, the teasing ended. Once we have learned to tolerate stress, its worst features dissolve away. So the mental and physical habit that we are breaking down is the bad habit of letting the alarm reaction take hold of us. If the habit can be broken at this point the pressure is decreased. This is not accomplished by an effort of the will. If we try not to get worried we take a tight grip on ourselves and this only increases the tension, with the disappointing result that the fear grows worse.

The art we have to learn is the art we had to learn at school when we were being teased; not to respond. 'Resist not evil', is the phrase in the Sermon on the Mount. Touch a taut violin string and it will go 'twang'; touch a man in a state of tension and he jumps. If we can relax physically and quite deliberately be a feather bed to everything that is teasing us, the situation begins to improve.

The point to grasp is that 'tension' is neuro-muscular tension: ie it is our muscles that are tense, not our nerves. We can learn to 'un-tense' these muscles by learning to relax; then, when we are feeling less strained; we can re-think what we are doing and how we can save ourselves from effort.

Relaxation: We must first learn how to rest, then how to stay relaxed and 'easy' even when we are working very hard. The first principle of relaxation is simple enough. My muscles (those which my will controls) work in pairs. When I pull on one, I stretch the other. I can test this for myself by stretching my legs out and pulling my toes up towards my calves. Then by doing the opposite – pushing my toes away from me – I relax the (reciprocal) muscle in my shins. The physiotherapist can demonstrate this in detail on groups of muscles all round the body. This relaxation technique is not difficult, but it does need practice.

To call this 'relaxation' is in fact slightly misleading, because it suggests rest and nothing else. The skill is to stay relaxed and use my body in a relaxed way. The athlete learns to relax, to make sure that he is not using any muscles that he does not need to use in the course of his very violent activity. Muscles use up energy and any waste of energy must be avoided; in fact, any muscle that is 'on', unnecessarily, is acting as a brake on his progress.

The second operation in 'de-tensing' oneself is to re-think one's mental attitude. Without some ability to relax, this is scarcely possible; so long as one feels 'driven' and at the mercy of what is going on, one cannot change one's behaviour patterns. (If I try still harder, I squeeze myself up still more.) The greatest gift of the human brain (it has been said) is the ability to pause: ie I can hold up the action, switch my mental approach, and not react as I first intended. This is particularly important in tension. There is a moment when I can feel the 'angry cat' or 'frozen rabbit' coming on, when I am just beginning to feel furious or frightened. By relaxing at that moment, I can say to myself 'nothing to be alarmed about', and switch to a more sensible reaction – the soft answer that turns away wrath, perhaps.

An example (often quoted) will make this clearer. The man in the firing line is under overwhelming pressure to hit back hard or to run away. If he cannot admit to himself how frightened he is, he has to go on fighting or his nerve would crack. He is the opposite of the very frightened man who goes to pieces, unless he has his back to the wall and cannot run any further. The man who is really brave knows how frightened he is, but he can accept his feelings and switch his behaviour, and so stand his ground.

At work or at home we see this frequently. The very rash have to unnerve the rest of us by the risks they take in order to be continually proving their courage; the temperamentally timid are just not there, for they are dreaming dreams of being somewhere else. But the bully has a soft under-belly (if one can only find it), and no one is so obstinate as the shy and retiring when they cannot retreat any further.

Meditation: The in-word at the moment is meditation. It has a very long history in the Christian Church, quite apart from its development in eastern religions. If the idea of meditation is now catching on, this may lead to a better understanding of how it works. Its physical basis is simple enough. Any idea or impulse that is going through the speech centre in my brain has an immediate, automatic effect on my body, on the set of my muscles, the state of my blood pressure or the secretions of my glands. In meditation the first essential is to relax, then to turn gently over in the mind some helpful word or phrase, like 'peace' or 'love', and let it sink (as it were) into the whole of one's being. For many people this is a very helpful, very liberating experience. When I am physically relaxed I unlock the deeper levels of my mind – my natural wisdom, if you like to call it that. It may be, as some physiologists are beginning to believe, that one side of my brain deals with everyday affairs while the other side supplies the long-term impulses and ideas which give me a course to pursue. I can only become constructive and creative and do something about my problems when I can relax and let this other side of me come to my help. I can then look beyond the difficulties and irritations of the moment, and regain some sense of perspective.

The quality of my life in terms of health, happiness and well-being, depends on the working of the inner core of my mind. I rely throughout the day (though I rarely think about this) on the steady flow of thoughts and ideas which well up as a 'stream of awareness' from somewhere inside me. I only know that when I am tired, I run dry: 'I haven't an idea in my head'. That is when I lose my ability to tackle the issues that matter and fall back on routine ideas and safe responses. When these turn out to be inadequate I then fall back on anger and fear. Unless I can find a way through, I am slowly but surely worn down.

The search for meaning: Meaning in life does not depend on a healthy body or a clever mind, but on that inner core of life that we call poetically 'heart' or 'soul', which represents everything most personal to myself. Is life just for nothing, or does it lead further? The deepest intuitions of religious thinkers (and artists and poets too) have said 'yes to life'. Christ believed emphatically that behind all the obvious mess and misery, love is trying to declare itself.

The essence of religious understanding is to take the process of relaxation and meditation one stage further. Sometimes rapidly, sometimes very slowly, the conviction grows that a deeper inspiration is taking hold of me. It may come as a deeper affection ('he that abideth in love, abideth in God and God in him'), or as a new stability of mind and purpose which carries us through great trials and leaves us enriched by the experience ('he whose soul is not upright within him shall fail, but the upright man shall live by his faith and sincerity'). Sometimes we have flashes of insight that show us the way forward.

Many religious people miss the way here because they think of faith as an effort of the will and belief as a dogmatic obstinacy. True faith is trust, which ripens into wisdom and spiritual strength. In fact it is impossible to trust with the mind unless the body is in a state of trust. The word for 'trust', which comes 46 times in the Psalms in the Hebrew Bible, literally means 'lying on the ground to renew one's strength', and the word for faith or genuineness, which comes so often in the Prophets, suggests 'standing upright and taking the strain'. The great Jewish writer, Martin Buber, said that for him these were the two poles of faith – to rest and let one's strength come back, and then to get up and get on with the job. It could hardly be better put.

Beyond psychology

The word 'faith', now has wrong overtones of meaning, and it is better to think in terms of 'trust'. This corresponds to the use in St John's writings of the word 'abide' – or 'stay put'.

Religion goes beyond psychology in its understanding of the basic idea of being oneself. To be oneself in ordinary speech suggests aggressiveness and exhibitionism, or the worst kind of self-expression. But this is a shallow unbalanced self, which is only part of the whole; a part that has to be 'denied' if we are going to discover the truth. It is equally true that the shy, withdrawing, 'self-denying' self of the unassertive is not the true self either; this also needs 'denying' or seeing through.

It may be worth pointing out that where Christ refers to the 'heart' as the source of everything evil, he means this incomplete self, for which our ordinary translation would be 'mind'. The seat of real feeling in Hebrew and Greek thought is below the diaphragm; one thinks at once of St Paul's 'I long after you all in the bowels of Jesus Christ'. As the saints and mystics remind us, the true self lies at a deeper level.

Here we are in a difficulty because Christianity has forgotten its original teaching about the Holy Spirit. Christ talked of a well of 'living water springing up into eternal life', and said that 'the Spirit shall be in you'. St Paul refers to the body as 'the temple of the Holy Spirit'. It has been pointed out that the Church of the first four centuries would never have sung a hymn beginning with the words 'Come, Holy Ghost', on the ground that the Holy Ghost has already come. The soul of man, liberated from spiritual bondage, was already enjoying this gift. 'He that abideth in love, abideth in God, and God in him'.

When we contrive to get past the shallow, one-sided false 'self' we have moments of understanding what all this means. As trust deepens and we are less dependent on our defence-mechanisms, these moments become established as a deeper insight. This is the long-term answer to 'stress'. This is marked by the recovery of a true balance inside oneself, and a deepening consciousness of Spirit.

The 'false self', as we have seen, is a matter of disposition, the limitations imposed by our early environment and by our subsequent failure to overcome those limitations. We go out into the world, part consciously and part unconsciously, as overlords or underdogs. This means that in any given situation, we cannot handle the situation as it needs to be handled. What we do is not what is needed but what we are forced to do by our own inner reaction. Where the situation demands a firm grasp or a quick decision we fail and break down, because we need to be directed and have our mind made up for us; where on the other hand the situation needs patience and delicate handling, we fail because we are ham-fisted spiritually and controlled by a compulsive desire to dominate or win every argument.

Because of our unconscious reliance on one side or the other of our defence system we go into life preparing in advance to run away or just spoiling for a fight. In either case we are basically unsure of ourselves and adding to the troubles of the world instead of solving them. 'To be all things to all men' (as St Paul meant it) is only a theoretical possibility, but most of us could do better – or rather, practise more accurately. The further we are towards becoming a whole person the further we have emerged from our false self, the better we are able to meet a situation on its merits. We do not have to meet a situation in a way that is laid down beforehand: we see, and do, what the situation requires.

When we are no longer compelled to satisfy our inner compulsions, we can breathe more freely. We are no longer emotionally at the beck and call of everyone who comes along, no longer at the mercy of the 'teasers'. We have room to manoeuvre, and to consider what our honest reaction to the situation really is. We can afford that *détente* which in the spiritual life we know as forgiveness, and remission of sins. We can afford to suffer constructively, because our suffering is going to help the situation. We can afford to 'let go, and let God' – and even set God free. We can accept others without our inner balance being upset in the process. We do not forgive them because we are obliged to forgive them anyway (which makes nonsense of the whole idea of forgiveness), but because we see their mistake and our own. We may even achieve heroism in forgiveness.

Our experience of Spirit is then that of a Centre (as St John of the Cross uses the word), as the source from which complete life, physical, mental and spiritual, springs. The source is open and we are refreshed. When we are trespassing on others by 'murdering' their lives, by cramping their freedom or denying their spiritual growth, or allowing them to 'murder' us, the mind is closed, in the state of darkness that the New Testament so often refers to, and there is no freedom of the Spirit. We are then 'walking in the flesh', says St Paul, meaning that we are physical and mental beings, and nothing more. When we are 'walking in Spirit', there is a unity of the whole personality which issues in 'fuller life'.

Another way of making the same point is to say that 'complete love' casts out fear. Complete love is rather like a horizon that necessarily recedes from us the further we advance in its direction. Our understanding of others increases as we work our way through our own weaknesses and failures, but more is continually demanded of us, and we are never more than unprofitable servants. Indeed, it is usually only through personal suffering that we come to realise our real weaknesses, which we are apt to mistake for virtues.

A common example will suffice: I 'sacrifice' myself (and if I don't say it, I often think it) to my family over a period of years, and I am dismayed to find that my wife or husband seems to grow more selfish every day and the children take every advantage of my kindness and are growing up into little hooligans. The catch lies in the word 'sacrifice', which in this context means 'propitiate, give way to superior force'. I have an inner compulsion to yield, and have made the best of a bad job by turning it into a virtue, labelled 'sacrifice'. No wonder my spouse and offspring are acutely uncomfortable; is there anyone more difficult to live with than the compulsively unselfish?

The same ambiguity surrounds the word 'suffering'. Our idea of suffering is usually running away from the kind of suffering which the situation demands and offering something else as a substitute. Much ill health is an escapist form of suffering, which we unconsciously find preferable to real life. In this matter too it is easier to preach than to practise, but life is a school which is continually forcing us to learn.

Truth making us free

This deeper awareness of Spirit becomes a more accurate con-science (in its original meaning of 'consciousness') as an inner urge to be true to oneself – to one's real self, that is, not to the false self which has proved inadequate. Religion is now so divorced from ordinary life that prayer and inspiration seem something apart, an exercise for people with time on their hands. But the whole purpose of special moments of spiritual recollection is that they are always adding something to ordinary life. We can coast along spiritually for long periods without them, and sometimes we may have to, but the growing edge of life will become very blunt. Prayer should be to the ordinary man what inspiration is to the artist, a process that gives him new vision; and new vision means simply that we come to old sights every day with clear eyes that each day see more and more. It is indispensable in any position that needs leadership and imagination, not least in the ordinary task of being a parent and running a home! Spiritual recollection should become part of the unconscious background of ordinary life where the wrong decision, by someone who has to make a decision, may have more devastating consequences than his sins. But we have a long way to go before clear sightedness becomes the mark of the Christian, and not muddleheadedness: it needs clear thinking and clear praying.

Real trust in God is largely a matter of honesty. It is only possible when we take God completely into our confidence. Set prayers are valueless when they are an excuse for evading real issues. It is honest to pour out to God everything that is filling one's mind, the hopes and fears, the doubts and uncertainties, the anger and hurt feelings, which anyone collects who is really trying to do something worthwhile in the world: the absence of such feelings may mean that one is just hibernating.

We need an inner baptism of love and reality, which washes off the stains of conflict: we can, of course, keep cleaner by keeping out of the conflict, especially if our defence mechanism is adjusted that way. But it is a spurious salvation. For most of us, life has to be met every day, and at the end of the day we need a time of recollection in which we can 'let go' the heat of the conflict and the dust of the marketplace. Some can form the habit of going over the day and seeing what lesson it has to teach; this can redeem even unpleasant experiences and make them profitable.

There is an area of life in which we all fail, and where our prayers could help us most. That is handling the person who rouses our worst instincts. Here we may be tempted to forgive or 'let go' much too easily. Whatever happens in the actual situation, in our prayers we need have no excuses and foster no illusions. We can be completely honest in the presence of God, and say and feel what we really mean. We shall come to understand the greatest mystery of all. Hatred is a perversion of love. We cannot in fact hate anyone in whom we have no interest. If we were not interested we should simply disregard them. If we hate, we secretly love and admire. If we can find out why, it is half the battle.

The other half is to discover that we cannot acutely dislike anyone who does not resemble ourselves in some unfortunate way. That can be the greatest discovery in life, if also the most humiliating. I hate someone who has the same vices and weaknesses as I have; I can see them all the larger in someone else, because I have 'a beam in my own eye' which obscures my vision. Hatred, accepted spiritually, opens up a new picture of love and understanding.

In short, the mind at ease is refreshed from deeper levels. 'Complete love' is creative; it takes the initiative and finds the way. We need not be so much on the defensive. As trust increases, as we cease to be afraid *for* ourselves, we are not so frightened *of* ourselves. Religion is not withdrawal from life, but real meeting with God and man.

CHAPTER TWO

Relaxation

The path to well-being

Introduction

Modern man has cut himself off from his roots. Continual striving for an objective that seems always to recede from him, leaves him strained and dissatisfied. He no longer knows what he wants, and he has no means of knowing, for he has cut himself off from the roots of his own being. The source of all life is within, but the result of such constant effort – always giving out and never taking in - is to empty more and more from the inner well of life without giving it a chance to fill: hence the emptiness and exhaustion of which most of us complain. Not only has this serious physical and emotional consequences, it deprives us of 'faith'

In fact, it gives us quite a false impression of the very word. Faith is linked in our minds with the idea of striving for the unattainable; or, to reproduce the schoolboy's howler, 'faith is believing what isn't really true'. This savours of magic and auto-suggestion. It is responsible for some of the worst excesses of 'faith-healing', in which the sufferer is worked up to an unbelievable pitch of emotional enthusiasm, with the inevitable re-action when the wave recedes. True faith is almost the reverse of this. It is a state of rest and receptivity, of 'abiding in God', as the New Testament suggests. When we read in the Gospels of being told to 'take up thy bed and walk' we are apt to think of the person concerned making a great effort: which shows how far we have lost the true tradition. The point of the story is that he suddenly discovered (through 'faith') that he could do whatever he needed to do, quite easily. Nowadays, owing mainly to our loss of spiritual insight, much more preliminary work has to be done before this 'faith' is reached, but the essential principle is exactly the same.

Our loss of insight is due to this yawning gap between the mind and the heart; in Pascal's words 'the heart has its reasons which the mind knows not of'. We cannot recover faith overnight, but we can let it grow again from within, and one of the simplest methods of doing this (particularly when we have no religion at all to start with) is to learn to 'relax'. The technique is simple, and anyone can learn it with a little practice; it may be best, therefore, to describe the technique first, and consider the spiritual consequences later.

Physical technique

We talk of 'nervous tension', but it is actually muscular tension. In ordinary life we never realise how tense our muscles are, though we may well know how difficult it is to rest. We should find it easier if we bore in mind one simple principle. The muscles that are under the control of the will work through the speech centre in the brain. When I think of moving my finger, the mere act of thinking immediately increases the blood supply to that finger, in readiness (so nature assumes) for the movement that will shortly follow. If I think of moving my arm, the added weight of blood in my arm can be measured in a laboratory. It is obviously useless to rest if we are thinking all the time of movement, or of what we ought to or might be doing, (Hence the frequent failure of a 'rest cure'.) But it is also true that, if we think rest, the state of the body will automatically follow our thinking. The art of relaxation, which is so much easier than most people imagine, is to talk (under our breath, for preference) to every part of our body in turn. This sounds ridiculous and, if done out loud, our best friend will doubt our sanity; but the fact that we are using the speech centre in the brain, means that relaxation will work – otherwise it may prove almost impossible. (The degree of concealed muscular tension that we habitually carry about with us has to be experienced to be believed.)

Sprawl in any comfortable position; it is easiest to lie flat on your back, in bed or on the floor, with a pillow or cushion to support the neck and, if desired, one under each elbow and under the knees. But good results can be obtained in a comfortable chair: it is only necessary that the body should be at ease.

Take a few breaths: just breathe in quietly and easily and let the breath go. Don't try for any particular effect: let your breathing come easily, without effort. Every now and then take an extra deep breath, yawn and breathe out with a little sigh. As you breathe out, just say to yourself, under your breath, 'I am letting go. For the moment I am letting go all effort and strain. I am not trying to do anything; I am just learning how to rest.' It is the easiest thing in the world to relax, provided that you don't try. (If you try to relax, then you are not relaxing.) Just let go and breathe easily. Any form of words will do, provided that the suggestion is always in the direction of release and letting go, never in the direction of effort and tightening up.

When you feel that you are breathing rather more easily, it will help you to form a mental picture of what is happening. Our 'life' is not our own: very obviously we depend entirely on the air we breathe, as one of life's essential components, and this air (or rather oxygen) has to travel through every part of the body, from the lungs, through the arteries, to each of the millions of the tiny cells which the body contains. Food, the raw material of life, is taken by the blood from the digestive organs, and the blood is charged with oxygen in the lungs, and is taken to every single cell, where the food is burnt up by the oxygen, and we are filled with energy. We are literally on fire all the time! The ash or residue is then brought back to the lungs and kidneys and disposed of. To do this, blood and lymph have to find their way through the tiny, hairlike capillaries in the muscles: if these are tense and squeezed up the process cannot occur easily, and dis-ease is the result. Relaxing all these muscles in turn will help considerably to ease the process of living.

This is the point. If your muscles are habitually so tense and contracted that this process is interfered with, the bloodstream cannot do its proper work. It is very much harder for the heart to pump blood through those tense muscles: when the muscles are relaxed, its task is much easier. It is also fairly obvious that if the muscles are tense, there are likely to be areas of the body which are physically below par. Instead of the body being cleared of its waste products, these accumulate in the cells. *We feel this as fatigue.* It increases our general vulnerability to disease. A little healthy exercise helps enormously to keep the circulation in good trim. Then when you feel tired, it is a healthy tiredness. You relax naturally, and the body soon comes back to normal.

Continue breathing in gently as before. As you breathe out, tell your fingers to 'let go'. Probably they will feel as though they were gripping or holding on to something; there is no need for them to be tightened up. Release them gently, stretch them out and whisper to them quietly to let go. When they feel looser and easier, say the same to your hands. You will be surprised to find how much the thought helps the action. The same with the forearm; while you are thinking of hand and forearm, ask yourself the question, 'Am I trying to fight anyone, or to ward off some danger or other? Am I meeting life with a clenched fist or an open hand?' Even if we are up against some personal opponent, or if we are faced with some problem or situation that seems too great for us, at least it will help to let the problem rest for the moment. So as you breathe out, mentally 'let go' all the problems and all opponents.

While practising breathing at the start of the exercise, it helps us to realise our dependence on forces and powers outside ourselves: we have to take in life day by day, or rather moment by moment, for life to continue. Recognising such dependence is one constituent of 'faith'; it is a comfortable feeling, and will grow if we let it. It may be helpful at this point to remember, and read again, such well-known passages from the Gospels as St Luke 12:22-34, or St Matthew 6:19-34.

While relaxing hands and arms we can think of two sayings from the Sermon on the Mount: 'resist not evil' and 'love your enemies'. Their meaning is inexhaustible, and we can only begin to understand them. When we relax, we automatically take up an attitude of 'resist not evil'. This is difficult to define: we feel our way into it, rather than work it out intellectually. It means facing and accepting our problems, whatever they are, and not seeking to evade them. We no longer tighten up and try to keep unwelcome feelings, or situations, or people, out of our lives. We let 'the tares grow with the wheat'. We shall grow into this very diffidently at first, but we shall find to our surprise that the attitude succeeds far better than we imagined. At least while we are relaxing, we can think tolerantly of our opponent. 'Love' is rather a strong word in English: kindness, tolerance, patience are the virtues we need. 'Kind' meant originally the attitude towards kith and kin, who are of the same 'kind' as we are; while we rest and let go, we can think of our 'enemy' as of the same 'kind' as ourselves. We can easily waste time on an imaginary enemy like the government, the income tax, or some foreign dictator; it is the person that we are really up against, who is making us tense. The attitude of 'kindness' is therefore one of trust, which is also part of 'faith'. As we let go and rest, we feel more tolerant and trusting (which does not mean that we close our eyes to things that are wrong; exactly the opposite – we open our eyes and examine closely what it is we have to deal with, which we can only do when we are relaxed).

When we come, in the same way as before, to relax the upper arms, shoulders, and back of the neck, we shall take a further step in the right direction by 'letting go' whatever burdens we may be attempting to carry. Many of us, without thinking about it, hunch up our shoulders as though (like Atlas in the fable) we were carrying the world. Talk to these muscles quietly, and help them to let go; let the shoulders fall and the burden roll off. We may have to take up responsibility again tomorrow, but it will help us to let it go for tonight. 'Sufficient unto the day is the evil thereof'. Do we need a new attitude towards our responsibilities? To think that we are indispensable is a subtle form of self-flattery to which most of us are prone. 'Let go and let come' whatever the future may hold: that may be a more constructive approach to our difficulties.

While relaxing the arms and shoulders, we can test how far we are succeeding by raising first the hand, then the forearm to the elbow, then the whole arm to the shoulder. Let it fall as loosely as it can. If it falls without hesitation, then our relaxation is good; if not, there is still tension which can be further released. A further sign of effective relaxation is a curious tingling in the fingers, which shows that the circulation is improving; and a general heaviness throughout the whole limb (which will eventually spread to the rest of the body). When we first begin to relax, we often feel more tired than we have ever felt before, as the pent-up weariness of years comes to the surface; it is all to the good that it should do so. Releasing the shoulders makes it possible to relax the back of the neck. This is a curiously important group of muscles; incidentally, the first that a baby can use. It is closely associated with the motions of pride ('stiff necked' or 'holding one's head up') and is particularly affected by suspicion (wryneck) and intolerance ('he gives me a pain in the neck'). It is a good plan to roll the head very slowly from side to side, like a heavy ball.

There is a sort of progression in relaxation: if we start with the fingers and hands and work back to the neck, we find our deeper emotions and attitudes coming to the surface. As we relax, we shall find it less and less possible to 'keep up an attitude' or pretend to ourselves that we are in some way different from what we are; we shall be able to let go our private dreamland, and let our dreams begin to find reality instead of our being severed from them; we then pick up a connection which we probably dropped in childhood.

The more we relax, the more we feel that we are becoming our natural selves. As the strain falls off, the tension begins to disappear. The result is a glorious sense of simplicity and freedom. A new peace begins to invade us, and we begin to feel more real; what is actually happening is that we are feeling much less false. This tendency will grow as we proceed. The general effect is one of quiet, if for the moment rather passive, confidence, which again is a necessary ingredient of 'faith'.

We proceed now to the face and head. Do exactly the same as before; talk quietly to the various muscles involved. There is no need to crease the forehead, for example. Our primitive ancestors may have tried to strike terror into their opponents by looking as frightening as possible, but it will scarcely help us. Nor is concentration much aided by frowning severely and squeezing up the eyes. Let go the muscles of the forehead and the cheeks, all round the mouth, pull back the tongue (its tip does not need support) then the muscles of the scalp and back of the head. Pay particular attention to the groups of eye-muscles. Imagine that your eyes are going to drop out of your head; they will not move in fact, but it will help to relax the eye-muscles. Very gently, without forcing anything, you can turn your gaze up somewhere above your head, then down towards your feet, across to the right and left, and then the diagonals; stretching the muscles will improve your vision. Many eye troubles start from our foolish habit of squeezing our eyeballs.

It is as well to practise the relaxing of the upper part of the body first. When you are satisfied that the accumulated tension there has been relieved, then turn to the lower limbs and trunk. Let go toes, feet, ankles. Help them to feel that they are on their own, as it were; they need a good rest, as they bear the burden of the body throughout the day. There is no need for chilblains, or cold feet; relaxation is an easy cure for both. We shall not suffer from cold extremities if we 'resist not evil' and lose our fear: more about this later. Let go the muscles all the way up the legs in the same way. Whisper to them gently and help them to release the strain. No need for cramp or varicose veins! Thighs and hips as well; they are probably easier to relax than hands and arms, but may not be so. The underlying problem here is likely to be fear, or in nature's language, the desire to run away or the wish that the floor would open and swallow us up. Many childhood memories of both these desires will probably come to mind. We shall stand much more sturdily on our two feet if we relax and let our legs do the work for us. Weakness in our lower limbs is due to a hidden desire not to stand on our own feet; if we admit frankly that we should prefer to rest, and take time to rest, our legs will take strength again.

As we relax, it seems as if our limbs are taking on a life of their own. The conscious mind is no longer trying to force the pace, and therefore all movement is accomplished with much less effort (and in consequence is more graceful). Our legs walk, with our mind as a silent partner, as it were. Athletes of the highest class have to practice relaxation, in order to give of their best. (Otherwise, as St Paul would have remarked, they will find 'another law working in their limbs' and cannot do what they will.) In a broadcast account of a recent Test Match the commentator remarked that a certain famous fast bowler was not yet giving of his best as he was not yet relaxed. If you watch first-class athletes on television, you will see them jerking their limbs about before a race, to make sure that there is no unnecessary tension anywhere. Why not do the same?

In relaxation the mind learns to co-operate with the body, instead of trying to dominate, control or force it. Relaxation as a preparation for childbirth is becoming standard practice and is robbing it of most of its pain and all of its terror. And what is true of the body is also true of the mind. We feel far happier when we learn to work with our mind at rest. A creative artist realises what is in his mind and gives the powers of fantasy full play; if he does not, the result is forced, artificial and uninspired.

It is a great help at the end of a period of relaxation to take advantage of the new freedom that our bodies have achieved by stretching vigorously, just like a cat waking up from a nap in front of the fire. Stretch the legs out as far as they will go and stretch the hands down towards the knees and let the whole body exult in physical freedom. The sensations of ease and power will then seem to go together naturally. At the same time breathe in deeply: imagine that you are holding a beautiful bouquet of flowers whose exquisite scent you are enjoying to the full. Then turn on to your front and get up gradually on all fours, without feeling that you have to tighten yourself up in doing so.

By this time our relaxation will be on its way to becoming an accomplished fact. At first we shall find that we tighten up considerably during the day, and need to relax in the evening. But as relaxation deepens, it will become a habit, and as we practice 'not resisting evil' we shall find that we can remain relaxed in action. Confidence thus grows from a passive to a more active attitude; we do everything more easily. We thus waste much less energy, and are less tired, or can do more, as the case may be.

Now as we rest and let go all the muscles of the trunk, we shall find a new warmth in the centre of our bodies, below the diaphragm in the region of the solar plexus. We can let this inner warmth spread all over the body, and encourage it by our thoughts as much as we can. We draw upon it when we need it; with a little practice we can slump for a moment in a chair and begin to feel refreshed. We are learning to draw thus upon the well of life within ourselves. Let go utterly and completely, and a deepening sense of warmth and affection begins to refresh the whole personality. Don't be discouraged if this takes time – a month or more. We all have a lot of bad habits to get out of, and they keep on re-asserting themselves. We endure a wholly unnecessary degree of 'neuromuscular tension' because we are so used to it, and we do not realise how much energy we are using up merely to keep our limbs in a set position! You may well despair of ever succeeding to relax, but it will creep up on you unawares and suddenly 'come'. (You had the same kind of experience when you learned to ride a bicycle!) The progressive uncoiling of the body in this way leads to a feeling of ease and naturalness. After years of feeling that tension was correct, it suddenly begins to feel unnecessary and wrong. We can let go the tension and do without it, first by learning to rest and then finding that we can remain relaxed even when we are quite busy. Once you get into the habit of relaxing, it becomes second nature.

Relaxing the mind

In your first attempts to relax you will still find yourself making efforts. One has to keep reminding oneself that trying and relaxing are different! If one cannot try to relax, how is it done? The answer is, a change in one's mental attitude. One of the positive gains of learning to relax is that it forces on one's attention many faulty attitudes of mind as well as of body. Relaxing one's body would hardly be necessary at all if one's mind had the right attitudes. But this does not strike us at first. The problem can be put quite simply. *No one can rest mentally and physically if he is fighting or running away.*

Why are our muscles so often unnecessarily tense? Why are we caught in this habit of not relaxing? The reason is simple enough. We are fighting somebody or running away from somebody (or a number of people). When I have something 'on my mind' it is a sign that anger and fear are working up. Anger and fear are two sides of the same coin. I only get angry because deep down inside I am a little frightened. Anger is one of the ways in which we keep down fear.

Look at it in this way. Anger and fear are a closed attitude to life. I am covering up and protecting myself, like a boxer with his fists raised. I am mentally on the lookout for a surprise attack. I am deeply suspicious of other people and their motives, and life looks threatening. So I am at the mercy of my over-anxious condition. This has obvious consequences. My digestion plays me up, my heart beats too fast, I am crippled with severe headaches or violent muscular pains, or I come out in a rash – and the doctor says 'it's nerves'. (That of course is the last straw.) This is a state of 'dis-ease': stress and strain are on the increase because we do not know how to cope with this state of affairs. 'Dis-ease' spells disease. So long as I am on the defensive, this is bound to happen. Only when I can let down my defences, can I know ease of body and peace of mind – which is what we mean by relaxation.

So we have to give up fighting and running away. We have to give up this closed attitude to life, which is playing us up so badly, and find an open attitude, in which we do not spend half our time putting up barriers against the rest of the world and hiding behind them and then complaining bitterly about loneliness and isolation! We will come to terms with life and make something of it - meet it and not resist it.

We have no word in English to express this! 'Acceptance' is probably the nearest we can get to it, although for most people 'acceptance' suggests 'giving in' But there is nothing in the least fatalistic about the attitude of intentional acceptance. 'No kidding' as they say: it means meeting the situation instead of running away from it. If I am not going to be ruled by fear, I must face up to my fears. 'What exactly is it I am afraid of?' If I keep asking myself this sane and healthy question, it stops my imagination running away with me. We all cross bridges before we come to them but many of our worst troubles never happen after all! 'What is the worst that can happen?' This puts a limit to my anxiety.

It also mobilises my resources to meet the situation. It is always worth remembering that curiosity is the antidote to fear. The more curious I can be, the less anxious I shall become. (Shyness can be sheer hell; but the shy person can go into a room full of people if he will be intensely curious about the shapes of their noses or the funny hats the women are wearing.) We reduce the problem to life size when we really look at it. Mountains shrink to molehills; we are no longer hypnotised by our own anxieties.

Mental relaxation means accepting the problem and taking a good look at it – in practice this often means taking a new look at it (or even looking at it properly for the first time). Relaxation is 'letting go' physically (and giving up one's physical bad habits).

When I take a real look at the problem, I can break it up into easy steps – in things I can do about it. If I look at an enormous room full of things to be cleared up or thrown away, my mind goes into a spin and the task looks impossible. But if I look resolutely at one little bit here and another little bit there, the problem begins to yield to treatment. This is true of all problems. (As the African proverb has it, 'if you want to eat the elephant in your path, first cut him up into small pieces'.) By facing difficulties in this way, we redress the balance in the nervous system. When I am problem solving, I switch from 'fight-flight' or paralysis by using my forebrain, central nervous system and voluntary muscles (especially my hands). I am once again in control of the situation, not controlled by it. I am no longer a frozen rabbit or an angry cat: I am back to being a human being.

It is even true of one of the most difficult problems that we are called upon to face – that of living with someone who cannot be loved! It may be a teenager who is at a very awkward age; or a member of the family who is having a nervous breakdown; or some elderly person who is slipping down into second childhood: or somebody at work who is difficult. Life is full of unhappy souls who need to get other people down, who are only happy when they can find something to find fault with, or who are 'mad' in the everyday sense of the word, even if the doctor gives them a clean bill of health.

Life is full of trying people (ourselves not excepted). We may well be afraid of them and we can try being angry with them, but it hardly ever works. By relaxing, we 'resist not evil'. If our temper is not roused, we shall not rise to their fly! If they know that we are not afraid of them, they will cease to try it on. But it must be genuine relaxation, and not just a pose (which everyone else sees through). If we are taut like a violin string, then our nerves go twang at the least thing that is said or done to us (even when no injury is intended). When we are not tense, the 'slings and arrows of outrageous fortune' do not affect us so deeply – at least, we recover quicker.

This is important, because we are all vulnerable in our different ways. Few of us can tolerate opposition or put up with outright antagonism. It is useless to pretend that we are not hurt. We have to accept adversity as part of our contribution to the general good. If someone (like the boss at work) is working off his feelings on us, perhaps his wife and children are not getting it as badly as they usually do! If I can handle so-and-so, it may force him to think again, and if he does not get away with it this time, he may think twice about it on the next occasion. The mental corollary of this is the breaking down of bad habits, and is apt to prove more difficult, just because it is the reverse of what we should expect. To achieve success I have been taught to try harder and harder. This has been elevated into a moral dogma. It would be much better to say what we really mean, which is 'try more accurately'. All of us have seen a man practising a golf shot or a tennis stroke, and making the same mistakes time after time. He is establishing the wrong habit as firmly as he can and regarding himself as a bit of a hero. *Much religious and moral effort is on a par with this.*

It is better to relax, give up the problem and come back to it with fresh vision, and perhaps with someone else's advice. But the basic difficulty goes deeper than this. We try too hard because we feel inadequate and know that we are wrong. Within us there is a sad distrust and a deep suspicion of our own ability, going back to demanding parents who wanted the child of their dreams to go ahead faster than the child could naturally go. Part of the healing of psychoneurosis is always to help the sufferer to understand the most important fact about himself – that his true aim is to discover and become himself.

The fact, therefore, that we know instinctively that something is wrong, does not mean that we should redouble our efforts to succeed – yielding in this way to the influence of our suprarenal glands – but to accept ourselves and find out what we really are and what we can do. It may mean accepting a target that is not quite so ideal, and not so far beyond our grasp.

It is strange but true that in our personal relationships if one 'is not trying' (in every sense of that phrase) the best course to take is often to do nothing. One is neither defending oneself nor attacking another, but merely standing one's ground. It is often better tactics, too, not to attack one's opponents directly, but to make it entirely clear what impact they are making on us: for instance: 'You are making me very angry', or 'are you trying to frighten me?' This has the advantage of opening out the situation, and it is not taken as a counter-attack. The gain on any one occasion may seem small, but the effect is apt to be cumulative.

More consideration can be given to personal relationships if one 'is not trying'. I cannot try to love my neighbour. I am caught in a false attitude immediately. If I cease to try, this is not the end of the relationship (contrary to what I might expect), but the easing of tension, which, in the long run, yields a big dividend.

Relaxing the inner mind

First, the body, then the mind: after that the deeper mind, which we refer to, poetically, as 'the heart'. A man can have a brilliant brain or a clever pair of hands but still 'have no heart', because something inside him has never grown. The inner mind uses the outer life for its own purposes, and when the inner mind is stunted, we find a 'wolf in sheep's clothing' or a facade with nothing behind it. The face of a beautiful woman can mask a spoilt child, and the executive ability of the tycoon may merely be a polite description for a petty tyrant at the controls. Behind a façade of professional competence may well lurk a frightened child. When we fall ill, we all revert to being frightened children!

Well or ill, we are often aware that we are living at two levels; the superficial everyday level in which I meet my friends and carry on my ordinary work, more from habit, perhaps, than from choice; and beneath that quite a different level, when my thoughts are subordinate to my feelings. These are more often concerned with myself than I should care to admit openly.

All too often I am crippled by hopeless feelings of failure, disappointment, inadequacy, jealousy, resentment and a whole lot more. In fact, all these are forms of fear, that corrosive poison which eats into mind and body and makes such deep inroads into health and happiness, undermining my courage and leaving me a helpless prey to all my weaknesses. But such is our desire not to 'lose face' that we will hardly ever admit that our real difficulty lies 'not in our stars but in ourselves'. We blame everyone else first.

The fact is, I am not yet free to be myself. I am a spiritual cripple who cannot completely grow up or live and feel as a real human being. I still think that 'the world owes me a living'. This prevents me from taking the responsibility for my own life, developing my own creative powers – doing anything in short but play for safety. But life is to be lived, not grumbled at, and there are always risks that have to be taken. By courageous living, I come into my own.

I am powerless to effect this change unless I let change occur. It is a process of spiritual growth, which can only happen gradually, as and when I make time for the real needs of living. I am resting and relaxing and refreshing body and mind: but something deeper than that is also happening. I might describe it as 'freeing my life'. I am unblocking the deepest resources that my inner life contains – the best word for it is 'inspiration'. When 1 relax my whole body and disengage my mind from its immediate worries and pre-occupations, I can feel a deep 'relief' that fills the whole of me. It is a curious feeling of recollection, of remembering and realising what I really am.

Religious people (in the truest sense of the word) have

described it for centuries as finding a centre inside oneself, which is the source and inspiration of everything in life that seems most worthwhile. Temperaments differ, and so does inspiration. One human being feels it as the filling of the mind and body with a deeper strength – power, life, healing are words often used to describe this. Another may feel it as 'belonging', especially those who have been through deep waters themselves and find a heartfelt sympathy with suffering, whenever they come across it. There are others, yet again, who find a tremendous sanity and wisdom in their deepest experiences, as a form of waking up to reality. This is the meaning of life; this is the clue that begins to explain everything.

But basically the experience is one of freedom. I am discovering what it is to be a real human being. Because I am no longer so afraid of myself, I can become more understanding and grow more tolerant. I no longer have to be right all the time – of all human traits surely the most difficult to live with – and I can both admit my own faults and accept the failures of others. I need not be so frightened and I need not be so angry. I am really becoming quite human!

That is what Christianity is about.

Spiritual Growth

Christ promised His friends 'eternal life'. 'I am come that they might have life, and have it more abundantly' (St John 10:10, Authorised Version); 'I came to give them Life, and something more' (Rieu's Version). He told the woman of Samaria, 'he that drinks the water I give him will thirst no more. The water I give him will become in him a spring of water mounting to eternal life' (St John 4:14, Rieu). 'If anyone is thirsty, let him come to Me and drink. He that has faith in Me shall, as the Scripture says, have rivers of living water streaming from within him' (St John 7:38). These phrases describe the feeling that comes to us as we learn to relax; it is precisely as though a well were being cleared within us, and the waters rising within the well. The sensation will grow until it includes the whole personality. At first it comes as warmth and vitality; later it will include truth and inspiration. A 'gift of healing', as practised in the early Church and in the churches of our own day, is the consciousness of this vitality rising within us and passing through us into the life of someone else. When the woman in the crowd touched Christ's clothes, He realised that 'power had gone out of Him' (St Mark 5:30).

By relaxing we discover our own inner life, and begin to enjoy the 'eternal life' that Christ was talking about. This means much more than 'future life'. It means Life, here and now, 'Life within oneself' (St John 5:26). At first this Life may seem but a thin trickle, but it will widen and deepen as we learn to accept it, understand it and use it. If we choose to follow it, it will lead us into the wholeness of Christian 'faith'.

As we relax, we think of Life outside us. If we are without any idea of God at all, it is easiest to start with the idea of Life in nature. We think of the life of an individual plant or animal, but Life is indivisible. Separate individual things are the channels through which the river of Life flows. The more we feel it flowing through ourselves and the more we can give ourselves up to its flow, the more kinship we feel with the world around us, the more kindness we feel for our fellow men. We can die to that

Life, or live to it .We can grow and expand in it, or contract and wither. We can feel health or sickness, ease or disease. We can help to build up the world around us, or we can help to tear it down.

But we have not yet achieved 'faith' in this Life outside us. That will grow, because there is in fact something which is both inside us and outside us, which is guiding us in that direction. We can fight it as long as we can: if we want all the pleasures of life and none of the pain, we exhaust the pleasures and find that the pain is still to come. 'In the Sermon on the Mount (St Luke 6 is the shorter version) Christ starts by pointing this out. Those are to be accounted fortunate who are experiencing the misfortunes of life, poverty, hunger, sorrow, and especially if these are incurred for the truth's sake. The opposites of these do not earn any spiritual reward. Life only becomes worthwhile when we break through the circle of our friends. 'Alas for you when all mankind applauds you ... If you love those that love you, what thanks have you deserved? Even sinners love the people who love them. And if you do good to those who do good to you, what thanks have you deserved? Even sinners do as much. And if you lend when you expect return, what thanks have you deserved? Even sinners lend to sinners in the hope of full repayment. No; love your enemies, be good to them and lend, despairing of no one – and your reward will be great and you will be sons of the Most High. For He is kind Himself to thankless and evil men. Be compassionate, like your Father. Do not judge, and you shall not be judged; do not condemn, and you shall not be condemned; forgive, and you shall be forgiven. Give, and you shall receive – there will be poured into your lap good measure, pressed down, shaken together and running over. For as you give, so shall you receive, measure for measure.' (St Luke 6:26-38).

The spiritual life, the life of fuller Life, means meeting life 'with an open hand instead of a clenched fist' (Graham Howe), not running away from what is unpleasant, but accepting everything as it comes, good and bad alike. 'Let go and let come'. This implies an attitude of physical relaxation, as we are beginning to realise. But 'faith' begins to quicken when it gradually dawns on us that it is not merely we on our side who are doing something.

As we are admitting Life, so Life is beginning to burst through; in fact it seems more and more that the initiative is with Life, rather than with us. As we learn to trust, so a Destiny begins to shape our end. Prayer begins (perhaps) through meditation; we begin to bring our doubts and difficulties into the presence of the Truth that seems to be emerging within us. The more we voice our doubts and turn them into words, the clearer Truth will become. We shall come to feel that Reality is 'personal'; in its wideness and vastness it has the 'attributes and qualities of that deeper 'self' which is beginning to break through in us. We may feel encouraged to be alone with this Reality; we can never believe in God unless we face Him alone. Something will happen to convince us that God is. So 'faith' begins.

Faith will demand forgiveness. We shall not be able to 'let go' and be as God intends us to be, if we are still clasping to ourselves some enmity against a particular person. To forgive someone is to 'let him go', to give up our demands upon him and not to seek the (possibly just) revenge that we are tempted to seek. This may be far from easy. It may be less difficult if we bear in mind that revenge so often hurts some third party who is innocent of the whole affair. (Jonah 4 is an illustration of this.) What will probably help more is the growing conviction that we are all wrongdoers and it is more humble to remove the plank from our own eye than the speck from someone else's eye.

Christ's view of it is given in St Matthew 18:21-35. Peter asks Him how often he is to forgive a brother – seven times? Apparently the religious authorities of the day suggested three or four times as the maximum: Peter must have thought that he was doing well to suggest seven. But Christ retorts that seventy times seven is nearer the mark, and gives a telling illustration. A king called a 'surprise check' on his accounts. One servant owed him a fantastic sum – ten thousand talents. He begged time to pay and his master forgave him and cancelled the debt. The same servant then went out and found another servant who owed him 'a hundred pence'. The latter similarly begged time to pay, but was refused and imprisoned for debt. When the king heard what had happened, he was furious with the first servant and imprisoned him instead. The sting in the story is the vast disparity between the two sums of money. The first is gigantic – Moffat translates 'three million pounds'; the second sum is paltry – £20 or so. In Christ's view God gladly forgives our debts to the tune of this vast sum, while we are unable to forgive the smallest debts against ourselves. 'So shall also my heavenly Father do unto you, if you forgive not everyone his brother from your hearts.'

'Relaxation' is thus a state of release, spiritual and physical.

The degree of release that can be won depends largely on how far we are prepared to follow the Truth, wherever it may lead. Locked up in the depths of the mind are many forgotten memories and repressed impulses. As release proceeds, these energies are unlocked. If we can with reckless honesty accept this other side of ourselves and bravely bring it to the light, we shall suffer an inner crucifixion – we shall indeed be bearing our cross – which will effectively undermine any spurious self-confidence that we may still possess. This is a real growth in spiritual honesty and reality. There is no room here for self-disparagement, still less for self-congratulation; both indeed are selfish attitudes, and neither will give new life. We have first to accept ourselves as we are, and then wait upon the Spirit within to heal us. That shadow, stunted self, our darker nature, with its repressed and explosive characteristics, will grow gradually to normal stature, if we give it time and encouragement to grow.

This is the greatest miracle of new life. The little self of our ordinary lives begins to be merged with the deeper self (or 'heart'), as we learn to accept and not to resist the promptings of our inner nature. Gradually, what lies in darkness is redeemed and brought into the light, and the rather pale, colourless light of our ordinary life takes on deeper tones and a more vivid hue. There grows an at-one-ment, or bringing together of opposites in our nature, as what is uppermost in our life is merged with what is lower. The 'higher' must not kill the 'lower', and the 'lower' must not swamp the 'higher'; they must grow together in love.

This inner process can only proceed in step with what is going on outside. We can only come to terms with our darkness within as we learn to understand our enemy without. Only by doing this do we come to a real relationship with God (St Matthew 5:45, St Luke 6:35). Our deep sense of unreality (including all our doubts and fears and worries) proceeds from 'negative' attitudes deep down in our lives; to attempt to redeem these feelings directly might well tear us to pieces. But if we turn our feelings outwards and discharge them through our prayers, a new life opens out for us. I can bring the enemy who has wronged me into the Presence of God.

I can let go all my feelings about him; the more childish my feelings, the more likely they are to be a genuine expression of what is in my heart! The more real my feelings, the more real God will seem to be; unless I am real, God cannot be real. As I let go my feelings, I begin to realise that all hatred is, directly or indirectly, hatred of God. One side of me therefore wishes to love God, the other to reject Him. I begin therefore to understand the deep spiritual truth that we have all crucified Christ. As I tell God how much I have suffered, one side of me will rely on His love and understanding to permit the other side of me to tell Him how much I fear Him, reject Him, and hate Him. Does that make sense? It will. The glorious spiritual paradox is simply this: the more I tell God what my other feelings are and the more I can live them in His Presence, the more clearly I know what St Paul discovered, that I am persecuting the Christ and re-enacting the Crucifixion. The Christ Who endured and suffered on the Cross all that the enmity and rage of man could do to Him; I cannot hurt Him by pouring out my darkest feelings against Him. If I do this honestly and completely, light begins to transfigure the darkness and, to my complete surprise, the darkness turns into some new, rich quality of the spiritual life. This is the mystery of the Cross, which transforms men's lives and fulfils them. 'As we are joined with Christ in His sufferings, so we shall rise with Him in His resurrection' (Romans 6:5).

As our life is thus redeemed from vanity and frustration, we begin to understand the deeper meaning of Christian symbols and sacraments. The image or representation of Christ is being formed in us (Galatians 4:19): we are growing to spiritual maturity: 'that ye may be strengthened with power through His Spirit in the inner man, that Christ may dwell in your hearts by faith; to the end that ye, being rooted and grounded in love, may be strong to apprehend with all the saints what is the breadth and length and height and depth' (all the dimensions of experience) 'and to know the love of Christ which passeth knowledge, that ye may be filled with all the fulness of God'. (Ephesians 3:16-19.) Or we can recall the message of St John's First Epistle (4:7-21): 'God is love; and he that abideth in love abideth in God, and God abideth in him', for we shall understand better what the word 'love' implies.

As we forsake our negative position of aloofness from the world at large and seek the fulness of life, we are letting ourselves go down into the water; the feeling is strikingly reminiscent of the idea of baptism. Christ regarded His Crucifixion as 'baptism'; going down into the depths is the way to new life. When we face our own darker nature, 'spirit' or 'fire' seems to be released within us. (Compare St Luke 3:16: probably in the Gospels 'fire' always carries the sense of purification rather than of punishment.) Much could be written on this theme. Through the deepening of our spiritual life, we are joined to Christ as branches to a vine (St John 15:1), and through the widening of our lives we find all experiences becoming the Bread of Life which Christ consecrates.

To be in communion with God, we have to share with Him the deepest experiences of our lives. We can turn our thoughts into prayers, and so enjoy the peace which defies understanding (Philippians 4:6, 7). By this means we admit the Spirit of Christ into the deepest recesses of our lives. It may help to focus our thoughts on the Cup. In our private prayers we can think of ourselves pouring into a Cup all our experience, and if we come together into the Presence of Christ at the Communion Service, we put into that common Cup not only our own lives but the lives of all about us. This sacrifice, giving to God and making holy, refreshes and renews us and recreates our spiritual life.

This slight sketch has attempted to show the relationship between ease of body and mind, and the intimate connexion between spiritual health and physical vitality. It may help to distinguish two ideas: the 'body and the 'flesh'. The body, as created and designed by God is a wonderful vehicle and expression of spirit; when it is functioning normally, it is whole, perfect and well. But we turn 'body' into 'flesh', the source of our weaknesses and temptations because we reject these weaknesses and temptations from our minds and 'repress' them. Unfortunately this does not mean that they vanish into thin air. Some of them we try to project on to others and make them carry our burdens for us, thus being the unconscious author of their weakness, or we submerge the feelings concerned into our bodies, so causing a physical deviation or distortion which we know as disease or strain. The process of physical relaxation releases strain and so enables 'flesh' to become 'body' once again. We are learning today that much physical disease has its roots in the emotional life of the sufferer. 'Relaxation' helps to release the problem from the body into the mind.

This means that the wisdom of the body can train and educate the soul. We can take, for instance, the side of the body against ourselves: 'why is this mind inflicting disease on me (the body)?' We shall then begin to see that our diseases reflect the pattern of our lives. A fearless acceptance of the situation will enable us to see how the situation has arisen. What do I not wish to see, so that I do not see? Or hear? What is it in life that I cannot swallow or digest? Why am I choking something back? Or cannot say what I really want to say? Why am I so 'stiff necked'? What is the cause of this inner rigidity that extends even to my limbs? Why am I so defeated that I lose heart? What is paralysing me? Why is life such a headache? Much food for thought here; and much thinking is being done by modern physicians along these lines. Much disease will be relieved if the underlying emotional problem can be brought out into the open, whether or not the actual problem can receive an answer: it is better to bear the cross and understand it than let it fall and cause ill-health.

'The Word 'became flesh' and dwelt among us,' Christians believe (for they have discovered by experience) that God has entered into every human weakness and limitation. Christ entered a good and evil world, suffering the evil and rejoicing in the good. 'The spirit is willing, but the flesh is weak'. Christ entered the very heart of evil on Good Friday, and 'flesh' became 'body' again on Easter Day. So our 'flesh' is becoming not only our 'body' but His Body. Whether it is our flesh that is diseased or our emotional life (our 'nerves'), we can believe that the healing Life of God, the Spirit of Christ, 'proceeding from the Father through the Son' can irradiate every part. 'Know you not that you are a temple of God, and that the Spirit of God dwelleth in you?'

(I Corinthians, 3:16, 6:19.)

CHAPTER THREE

Be
Not
Anxious

Meditations for
nervous sufferers

1. The presence of God

'In Him we live and move and have our being.' (St Paul)

Sometimes we feel that God is very near, sometimes that He is very far away; the hurry and bustle of everyday life seem to come between us and God and form a barrier which we find difficult to break down. But there is no reason why this should be so. We have to concentrate on what we are doing; but we need not for that reason lose the sense of God's presence.

There are two things we can do to help us over this difficulty, and once overcome the difficulty will not return.

First, in a time of quiet meditation, think of the presence of God as being everywhere – 'in Him we live and move and have our being'. Then, very slowly and deliberately, with that thought in the back of our minds all the time, pass through the mind everything that we do in the course of the day – everything, however trivial it may be, from the moment we wake up till the moment we go to sleep at night; this helps us to realise that wherever we are, whatever we are doing, we are quite as much in the presence of God as when we are saying our prayers.

I remember once, many years ago, thinking how difficult it was in all the varied things one had to do in the course of the day, to keep one's sense of the spiritual. Then I realised that the effort and strain of trying to do so were quite unnecessary. We are not trying to cling to God; we are asking God to take care of us, and if we are content to leave the spiritual problem to Him, we get on twice as well with half the effort.

'O Lord, Thou knowest how busy we must be this day; if we forget Thee, do not Thou forget us; for Christ's sake. Amen.'

The spiritual sense which we gain through our prayers can be brought into our daily lives if we bring our daily lives into our prayers. Many Christians try to lift themselves up to God's level – try to climb up to Heaven as it were. But the message of Christmas is that God came down to earth; and the sooner we come down to earth too, the stronger and more practical our faith will be.

Our spiritual life has its mountain tops, but the work has to be done on the plains. We need to take our spiritual life with us into the world where it can do some good to others as well as ourselves.

Life will become spiritually much more real by some such simple meditation as the foregoing. If we pass through the mind the sort of things which we do in the course of the day and realise that the presence of God is always there as the background of our lives, we shall find this a great source of spiritual strength.

2. The image of God

God cannot come into our mind until we admit Him; we cannot have faith in God while we still think of Him as a very remote, far away being who has no direct contact with our lives. When we form a real friendship with somebody, the basis of this friendship is an exchange of confidence; your friend trusts you and you trust him; without this mutual confidence there is no friendship. It is the same with our prayers: to have confidence in God, we have first to give Him our confidence. God cannot put His faith and confidence in us unless we first acknowledge our troubles and difficulties to Him.

But before we can do that – before we can feel like doing that – we must have the true picture of God in our mind. Christ told His disciples that if they had seen Him, they had seen the Father who sent Him; we have not seen Christ, but we can form a picture of what He was like by thinking of some of the things He said and picturing what He was like in His graciousness.

'Love your enemies, pray for them that persecute you ... judge not, condemn not, forgive, be merciful.' If Christ said things like this to His disciples, He must have practised them Himself. It is this picture of Christ that all down the ages has drawn men to Him. They have felt that there was someone who completely understood. One would have complete confidence in the presence of such a man as that; and if Christ was like that, so was the Father who sent Him.

'There is no place where earth's sorrows
Are more felt than up in Heaven;
There is no place where earth's failings
Have such kindly judgment given . . .

For the love of God is broader
Than the measures of man's mind;
And the heart of the Eternal
Is most wonderfully kind.'

'Almighty God, unto whom all hearts be open, all desires known, and from whom no secrets are hid; cleanse the thoughts of our hearts by the inspiration of Thy Holy Spirit that we may perfectly love Thee, and worthily magnify Thy Holy Name, through Christ our Lord.'

3. The release of anxiety

'In nothing be anxious, but in everything, by prayer and supplication with thanksgiving, let your requests be made known unto God; and the peace of God, which passeth all understanding, shall guard your heart and your thoughts in Christ Jesus.' (Phil 4:6-7)

We find it very hard, sometimes, to concentrate on our prayers. We no sooner begin to say them than our minds leap off on to something completely different, quite trivial and irrelevant probably, which has nothing to do with what we really mean to pray about.

Have you ever seen a child which feels lost and left out of things? He comes and pesters his parents and the people round him, because he feels neglected and wants to attract attention. The other side of our thoughts is rather like that, as we shall see.

It is a great help from time to time to bring these straying thoughts into our prayers instead of trying to keep them out; in fact, we shall enlarge our spiritual vision considerably if we do.

We start by saying a quiet prayer to recall the presence of God, and then let the mind roam just where it pleases. Very likely it will lead us to some very foolish little anxiety, in itself so trivial that we are probably ashamed to think that we worry about it at all. But now we take it seriously; we start by confessing that it is an anxiety; we acknowledge it in God's presence, surrender the whole problem to His care and ask Him to help us not to worry over it further 'Sufficient unto the day is the evil thereof' and it is no use adding tomorrow's worries to today's.

By letting the mind roam on in this way, we shall be surprised to find how many small worries we are carrying about in our minds all the time. They all tend to sap our nervous energy, and we would feel much better without them.

Now this is the important point: if we take these first anxieties seriously, they will lead us deeper down to other anxieties which matter far more. Our thoughts are arranged in layers, as it were; usually we are only conscious of what we feel on the surface and have little idea of what is going on underneath. This other side of our thoughts is rather like the neglected child which feels out in the cold. Just as the neglected child clamours to be taken seriously, and is always inventing excuses to attract attention to itself, so this other side of our minds, which is usually shut out of our prayers and our daily lives, is always inventing excuses to attract notice by filling our minds with trivial worries and anxieties which in their way are quite unreasonable. They get into our prayers, stop us from sleeping easily, and take all the joy out of life. That is why we have to take them seriously and find some way of *releasing* them.

We can do this most easily by turning them into prayers. That is what St Paul meant when he told the Philippians not to be anxious about *anything,* to 'let their requests be made known unto God', then the peace of God would come into their minds. When we acknowledge our hopes and fears to God we take God into our confidence. We give God the chance to strengthen and renew our faith by putting His thoughts and ideas into our minds. Obviously, on the other hand, if we keep a large section of our thoughts out of our prayers, then our faith in God will be to that extent incomplete. It is only when our hearts are open to God that we can have faith in Him.

The release of anxiety, therefore, is to turn cares into prayers. If we feel anxious about somebody, that anxiety does no good to us or to them. But if that anxiety is turned into a prayer, it widens and enriches our spiritual life, it turns a thought which is depressing into a thought which is uplifting, and it also helps the person we are praying for.

4. Resist not evil

The picture of the naughty child in the nursery is a very helpful one when we are considering the problem of 'nerves'.

So often the rebellious child is the child who feels neglected and left out. The same is true of our thoughts. An anxiety is like an aching tooth; we can shut it out of our minds for a time by a great effort of the will by concentrating our attention on something else; but directly we begin to get tired, the pain returns – usually with redoubled force! It is the same with our anxieties; we can control them for a time, but only for a time. The more we fight them, the worse they become. (There is a good reason for this.)

But why fight them? What is the best way of controlling a naughty child? If you are angry with it (or 'fight' it) you make the child naughtier than ever (and you will get tired before the child does). If you are wise, you will try different methods: disregard the child and let it see that its naughtiness is not disturbing you, and then give it something useful to do.

We can do the same with our thoughts if we 'resist not evil' and treat the anxiety (or whatever it is) in the same way as we should treat a naughty child. Don't give in to it, don't let it annoy you; don't attempt to fight it; just relax and let it do its worst. You will then find some way of making use of it.

Behind the thought that is worrying you there is some lesson which God wants you to learn. Turn the anxiety into a prayer by asking God what is the meaning of it. That is the only way to win permanent spiritual harmony and peace.

'Lord of all being, I confess to Thee I am unable to control or overcome this worry (anxiety, fear...) without Thy help. I bring it to Thee as part of my unworthy self and ask that it may be consecrated to Thy service. Explain to me what it means, that I may turn it into a thought that is worthy of Thy love.'

Remember one thing – when you are plagued with thoughts that you cannot control, God is just as near to you as He always is. You may think that you have lost Him, but He has not lost you. God is taking care of you, not you taking care of God. Just believe that through the fog of worry and doubt God is leading you to a greater peace than you have had before. He can't do this unless you make the venture of faith and follow Him through the darkness until you reach the light. We can adapt a well-known collect that St Benedict asked his monks to say every evening:

'Lighten our darkness, we beseech Thee, O Lord, and by Thy great mercy defend us from all the perils and dangers of our spiritual night.'

5. Complete acknowledgement

Sometimes our minds just stick: no other word will describe it. The same thoughts go round and round in our head, or no helpful thought comes into the mind at all. We seem unable to 'get through'. We cannot escape from ourselves and the vicious circle of self-centred thinking.

Tell God exactly what you are feeling and thinking. Offer no excuses, waste no time in regrets; merely come to God and say exactly what is in your mind. Confess your doubts to Him too. Say exactly what is in your mind even if it concerns others whom you normally love and trust. If you are feeling bitter, spiteful or resentful, don't keep these feelings out of your prayers but tell them to Him who understands all things.

God's way of healing is to sow the seed of something better in the depths of our minds, and as that seed grows in us, so it pushes up into our minds everything that comes between it and the light of day; like a tiny plant can uproot a paving stone by continually pushing it upwards, so the seed-thoughts in the depths of our minds will push and push till they have pushed everything else out.

If we banish these unwelcome thoughts from our minds, we merely hinder the process of healing. They are forced into our minds in order that we may take them out of our minds and give them to God. The more we give God what is in our minds, the more room there is in our minds for what He wants to put in them. There is no need for us to search our minds; merely (as someone has put it) to skim off the scum as it rises to the surface.

'O Lord who has taught us that there is nothing hidden which shall not be revealed, grant us to offer to Thee all things in us which are contrary to Thy Will.'

'Whatever you ask for in prayer, believe that you have

received it, and you shall have it' (Mark 10:24)

When our minds are so tired and confused that we can no longer think out our spiritual problems, we learn to leave them in the care of God and thank Him that we have already received the answer to our prayers and the solution of our difficulties. This is a test of faith. If we really believe in the Love of God, we shall say a little prayer of thanksgiving, and go on with our work if we are well enough to do this, or rest if we are not. Then at some moment of the day when we are off our guard or not thinking of anything in particular, the thought that we need will come into our minds, and we shall feel that God has spoken to us.

6. The indwelling spirit

'Wait thou silent upon God' (Ps 62:5).

'He that abideth in me, and I in him, the same beareth much fruit' (St John 15:5).

To understand what our Lord means, we must practise our 'abiding in God'. So many people feel that God is very far from them, and that they must make great efforts to reach Him. But the Christian knows from experience that the Spirit of Christ is abiding in him. It is when we cease to strive and strain that we realise this. Like Martha we are worried about many things; like Mary we find peace in the Master's Presence.

We learn to rest in God by practising rest. It is a great help to lie down flat on our backs – one can practise this in bed – and let our bodies relax. We breathe in quietly and gently and as we breathe out we 'let go' all effort. True relaxation consists in not trying; simply giving up all straining and striving and leaving everything to God. As we rest in this way, we feel at first a mere lifelessness, but as our sense of rest and trust deepens, we are surprised to find a new strength gathering within us. We can assist the process by spiritual meditation. The word 'spirit' means breath, and as we breathe in we can pray that we are receiving the Spirit of Christ; that 'eternal life' is being carried to every part of the mind and body, cleansing and renewing every bone, every muscle, every cell. Each day we can renew our inner life in this way, and feel that the power of God is being released within us. (This practice of rest and relaxation can be combined with sections 3-5.)

We then realise the great truth as so emphasised in St John's Gospel, that we have eternal life within us.

Christ said: 'he that believeth in Me, hath eternal life' (St John 5:24). It is not a gift in the future, but a gift that all enjoy here and now. Think also of what He said to the woman of Samaria (4:14): 'eternal life' is the constant theme of this Gospel (eg 3:36, 5:54, 7:38, 10:10, 11:25-26, 17:2-3, 20:22).

'O Lord Jesus, who didst promise Thy disciples the gift of eternal life: grant us day by day to rest in Thee, that our strength may be renewed, and that with Thy love in our hearts and Thy life in our bodies we may so carry out Thy will and intention that thereby we may fulfil our heart's desire, to Thy honour and praise and glory.'

7. The world outside

As Baron von Hugel once put it, if we ask for the grace of God we must give the grace of God something to work on. We are far too prone to come apart from the world and enjoy our little spiritual happiness with God – and then are surprised one day to find that the well of inspiration has dried up and our prayers seem 'dead'. How could it be otherwise? 'If ye love them that love you, what thanks have ye? Even sinners love those that love them'. If we are to be in tune with the love of God, we must bring into our prayers, and into our lives, the people we dislike.

'Love your enemies . . . pray for them who despitefully use you and persecute you': that was our Lord's advice, and if we followed it more literally than we do, a great many of our unreasonable fears would begin to subside. To mention only one point, if we make a habit of praying for people we dislike, we are immediately less annoyed with them and less afraid of them, and half the battle is won already. It is surprising, too, how often we find that the fault is on our side, that the beam is in our own eyes, and what prevents them from giving us the goodwill which we should normally expect them to give, is something in us that repels them and turns them away.

Pass through your mind a few of the people (or types of people) whom you usually find it difficult to get on with. Bring them into the presence of God in your prayers and pray that they may dislike you as little as you are trying to dislike them: pray that they may have the spiritual enlightenment which you enjoy and that you may have the spiritual enlightenment that they possess – it all helps. (You wouldn't feel jealous of them unless you felt, underneath, that they had something which you haven't, and that they were right, in some way, and you were wrong.)

'O Lord Jesus Christ, Who didst come to break down the

spiritual barriers that separate one man from another, help me to grow in wisdom and sympathy and to see all men, my friends and enemies, in the true light that comes from Thee, that I may be protected from false friends and may find new friends among those I dislike, and so go forth into the world with courage and boldness and freedom from fear, in Thy Name.'

8. The gospel of forgiveness

'When ye stand to pray, forgive, if ye have aught against any'.

Christ did not tell us to confess our sins to God; He told us to do something much more practical – to forgive our enemies. How many nervous sufferers would be saved endless spiritual trouble if they would only do this. By chaining our enemies to ourselves, as it were, by brooding over our feeling of being wronged, we keep our troubles always with us and there is an inevitable feeling of spiritual strain. What we are to aim at is spiritual release.

This is very far from being easy. If the wound is very deep it needs much prayer and spiritual insight on our part before we can say, 'Father, forgive them – they did not know what they were doing', or 'they did it for the best'. But we must learn at least to take the first step, which is to pray for them. If we bring them into the presence of God, Who is all-wise and all-loving, then the burden is lifted off ourselves

Perhaps we can go further than this. St Augustine said that if Stephen had not forgiven Saul of Tarsus, Saul would never have had the experience on the road to Damascus which made him Paul, the great missionary to the Gentiles. There is a lesson for us here: as we pray for those who 'despitefully use us' or who are not being fair to us, we are helping in their spiritual salvation as well as our own. The Christian Church would be a much greater spiritual force than it is if it consistently practised the teaching of Christ about the forgiveness of sins.

In many cases of nervous suffering a scar (as it were) has formed over the wound and we no longer realise that we still feel its effects. It is not necessarily wise to reopen these old wounds. But if we take the matter to God in our prayers, He will reveal to us what is the matter – provided that we have the faith to follow wherever He seems to lead.

Again and again our spiritual difficulties are very much increased by our failure to forgive our enemies. We may have so far lost the joy of life that we do not really want to get well: this is nearly always due to some very long-standing difficulty with someone who is fairly close to us. Chronic jealousy, self-centredness and a sense of persecution are nearly always due to this same cause. It is no use asking the help of God to release us from these difficulties unless we first release those that err against us.

'Forgive us our trespasses, as we forgive them that trespass against us.'

9. Spritual loneliness

Perhaps the hardest feeling of all to bear in anxiety-states is the feeling of being cut off from all other human beings. We feel so desperately alone. We are apt to imagine that no one else has felt as we do – needless to say, that is quite untrue. Sometimes the whole of our affection seems to go quite dead. We go on behaving as though we still had our natural feelings;

inwardly, however, we feel ourselves to be hopeless hypocrites, and something inside us warns us that we are only keeping up appearances or playing a part. We long desperately to do something to help others; but whatever we do, the same contemptuous voice within us continues to remind us that we are not serving others but merely gratifying ourselves. We can never escape from this intolerable feeling of 'self'.

Most people feel that they are going completely mad when this happens, but it is a very ordinary symptom of tired nerves. One half of us is still thinking about the outside world and its needs, the other half is obstinately centred on ourselves. The first thing to do is to accept this for what it is – a natural state of affairs. If something within us is compelling us to think about ourselves, that is Nature's warning that something in ourselves badly needs thinking about, in the same way as an aching tooth warns us of decay. Nature forcing us to think about ourselves is the reason why, for the time being, we feel so cut off from the rest of mankind. We have to have faith to believe that God is working His purpose out through the working of our own minds, and ask Him what He is trying to do in us and what lesson He wishes us to learn. Deep down below all this turmoil and distress lies the answer to our problems. We have within us a well of living water, but we can't get to the water because of all the rubbish with which we have succeeded in blocking the well, and the only thing to do is to let God take the rubbish out. Thus if we continue to turn our troubles and difficulties into prayers, we shall feel that the help which God is sending us is finding its way through.

It is a great help to pray for others. If we feel that there is a barrier between us and other people in ordinary life, we can at least feel with them in our prayers. In order to escape the feeling of 'self' pray particularly for people who are estranged from each other. There are people all around us who are in great need of this particular prayer: husbands and wives who can't get on together, parents who are at cross purposes with their children, people who get on each others' nerves at home or at work. Many of them need our help very badly, and we are helping in God's work in the world if we pray that they may be reconciled to one another. 'Blessed are the peacemakers . . .', there is great need of makers of spiritual peace.

In such a prayer there need be no emphasis at all on ourselves and in praying such a prayer for others we shall help to make peace between the warring elements in our own souls. Little by little the sense of separation between us and the rest of the world will disappear. It is just as if there is a series of veils between us and people we know – some sufferers even have the feeling that people they are talking to are not really there – but as God restores us to inner harmony and peace, these veils are removed, one by one; we feel the presence of other people once again, and natural affection returns.

'O Lord Jesus Christ, Who didst come to preach peace and goodwill amongst men, we pray for the blessing of Thy love on ... and ... that they may be reconciled to one another and may live in brotherly union and concord, forgetting pride and vanity and seeking only to serve each other in order to serve thee, Who with the Father and the Holy Spirit livest and reignest in perfect Love, one God, world without end.'

10. Fulfilled with joy

'That your joy may be fulfilled' (St John 16:24).

Joy implies enjoyment. If we are to understand Christ's promise we must learn to accept life, to love life, and to enjoy life.

This means 'becoming as a little child' (Matt 18:3). A healthy child is very curious, extremely practical, full of common sense, is naturally friendly, and enjoys abundant life! That is what we should be, if we really believe the good news about Christ.

Be curious: the natural antidote to fear is curiosity. Practise your curiosity by going for a short walk and seeing how many things you can see that you have never noticed before. If you have to go into a room full of people, make up your mind what you are going to be curious about – eg the shapes of their faces.

Enjoyment: that also needs practice. Waking up in the morning and thinking how awful the day is going to be, is to accept defeat before we start. Think instead of all there is to enjoy in a new day. Make up your mind to enjoy it as the gift of God, and help others to enjoy it too.

Practical common sense: be constructive, and don't waste time and nervous energy on imagining things. The more firmly rooted our feet are on the solid earth, the less we shall be likely to be haunted by nervous fears.

'Grant, O Lord, day by day that we may enjoy life as Thy heavenly gift and encourage others to abandon all unworthy fears and to make the most of all that Thou dost give us.'

CHAPTER FOUR

Dependence
and
Independence

This subject is a fundamental problem which we all have to face, both in our own lives and in our dealings with other people.

A typical example is the conflict between 'what I really want to do' and 'what other people think I ought to do'. It is the central problem of all psychoneurosis and many physical or 'psychosomatic' diseases, and many practical problems of behaviour. When do we assert ourselves and get our own way, with all that that implies? And when do we give in to other people? So often the question arises: 'What is the will of God for us, and how are we to interpret it?' It also occurs in an acute form because so many of us were brought up in a Christian atmosphere and have become strongly biased towards one solution or the other of this problem, and not necessarily the best or right solution. People say: 'Am I being selfish over this?' or 'should I be less selfish?' To the question how often one should assert oneself, the right answer may well be 'not often enough'. When I think I am being good or kind or unselfish, how often is that a weakness rather than a source of strength, a hidden vice rather than a virtue? And how often does it rather undo God's intentions instead of fulfilling them and expressing them?

If you turn the problem over in your mind you will realise how far reaching this basic conflict is: self-assertion or withdrawal, selfishness or unselfishness. It expresses two sides of human personality; it is not just a problem which arises in some lives in an acute nervous form, but a basic difficulty of human nature. We can see this by taking an example from a different field. The Russian scientist Pavlov used to classify his dogs by their reaction to clicking his fingers; one type would pay attention, another would not. The dog that paid attention easily was liable to be highly-strung and nervous; the one who paid no attention and went his way, would never be highly strung and would never be obedient. This was true basically in the constitution of the dog; the one who attended easily would react quickly to a simple sedative, whereas the other might require eight times as large a dose.

We are broadly divided into these two classes; those who are receptive (through their nervous systems) and those who are not receptive (they are the assertive ones). The two types are known by many names, such as introvert and extrovert; William James' descriptions of 'tender' and 'tough' are as good as any. Whatever you call them, the basic underlying difference is the same throughout history. The more sensitive natures are often those who take more easily to the religious life, are more receptive spiritually and understand better the things of God: whereas to make an impact on the world requires a tougher kind of human nature. The difference also exists in ourselves, for even the 'toughest' person after a long illness becomes more tender, more receptive, more willing to accept - but it may not last!

Sensitive people are frequently dependent and often brought up to think of the religious man's dependence upon God as a virtue, as part of the religious life (which it should be). You have, however, only to think of the enormous number of such people we know - for we can always see other people's failings so much more easily than our own! - to realise that their dependence upon God is often a source of weakness to them and not nearly so much a source of strength as they would like to imagine. Sometimes people who are called 'pillars of the church' are not so much pillars as buttresses; they just lean, in fact they positively cling! There are a great many who regard themselves as good Christians, (and they may well be) but no one can say that they are grown-up!

So often our religion is an escape from reality and we tend to run away from life, and that is a poor reason for faith and trust in God. We do not find it easy to see through this particular difficulty. At the back of our minds, so often, we have the thought of salvation as an escape from reality, always begging to be saved from something. I do not believe that religion can be described as escape from anything; we should really pray to be saved not from difficulties and trials in the world but through whatever difficulties may come our way. The true example of the Cross is that we are carried through the darkness and suffering until we come to the light, and the trial or the trouble is the gateway to something better. If we are depending upon God, it is to be saved not from life but through life; and the more we think about that distinction, the more important it becomes. Many people would be a great deal stronger physically and spiritually if they put this into practice.

What do we mean by 'independence'? Standing on our own feet? It is easy to see in this case what the difficulties can be. We all know people who have battled against life very bravely for a long time, and eventually they have tired themselves out and exhausted all the people round them. To the end they were determined to be independent, but with it went a tremendous amount of pride and self-exaltation. They tried to climb up to heaven, and as they seemed to get there, it receded from them; the more effort they made, the more it withdrew.

For people of this kind – and for this side of ourselves – success is fraught with new disappointments, and they look back with a certain degree of bitterness and disillusion. They had their ideals; they have done their best to fulfil the laws of God and the purpose of Christ, but they get very weary, disappointed, and go downhill physically. Even if one is a pillar of the church and not a buttress, it is not the end of this particular problem; and mental and physical strain is directly caused by the failure, so common to us all, to find a solution. That part of the involuntary nervous system which the doctors divide into sympathetic and parasympathetic, expresses these two main sides of the personality. When we are standing on our own feet, grappling with the problem, the sympathetic nervous system is bringing our fighting spirit into play, exciting most of the organs of the body, and living life faster than nature intended.

When the opposite tendency, the drive for dependence, comes into play, it brings the other side of the nervous system into activity. It produces an intense feeling of weariness and lassitude, a great desire to withdraw. Most of us do not understand that our feelings of weakness, or being terribly tired or terribly inadequate, are not just the absence of something, that our strength has faded out – nature does not work that way – it is a see-saw; when this side comes into operation, it is a different part of the body. So do not pray so much for strength; try to solve the problem, try to find why the see-saw has tilted up that way. The apparent weakness is a force (nervous and chemical) and you must find out why it is working. It feels like weakness but do not reproach yourself, feeling that you have failed or lost something; something is working in you which God designed, and your problem is to find out what it is, and why.

You will now see how basic this difference is, and you will also understand that if you are constantly fighting, you will be liable to a certain range of diseases, on the output side, affecting heart and lungs and muscles. If however you err on the dependent side, it is the receptive part, like the digestive apparatus, which may be affected.

What did God want to bring out of all this? Quite obviously we should progress through many different stages, in which these alternating aspects should play their appropriate parts.

We start life in a state of utter dependence, and gradually grow into independence, and we should recognise how frequently these two phases alternate – we try to walk, and tumble down, and try again. What nature is working out through all this is that we should be instinctively preserved by the 'dependent' side of ourselves from the false choice of pursuing a particular line of action too far. What we should grow into is both dependence and independence, and the ability to use the two sides of ourselves alternately.

It is true, I believe, that the two Hebrew words for 'faith' in the Bible represent these two sides of our life. The word that occurs about 50 times in the Psalms represents lying down on the ground; that is, complete dependence and complete trust, partly (no doubt) because lying down was one of the most ancient attitudes of prayer. Complete dependence on God, therefore, might well be symbolised by lying down on the ground, simply resting on mother earth, waiting still upon God, trusting our whole life to the activity of God, without ourselves getting in the way to the smallest degree; completely receptive, completely dependent. The other word for faith, so frequently found in Isaiah, represents standing upright firmly, and this should be the second stage; when we have learned to be completely dependent, we can learn to be completely independent. Our whole life, little by little, will then be in the process of manifesting or expressing the nature of God in our lives, so far as we have been able to receive it. We lie down, rest and relax, in order to be able to stand up and express in the world whatever God will put into our minds.

Another way of describing this is by taking in and giving out, receiving and expressing, drawing in and breathing out. There must be this rhythm in our inner life, which thus governs and controls the whole personality. If we stick on one side or the other, something goes wrong. Most of us are trying too hard, and we have forgotten how to take in, so that we run short of love and life, and run dry. We need to take in as well as give out.

When we come up against a problem or a difficulty, whether of healing or of ordinary life, it helps so much to remember these simple basic rules. We are faced with a problem: the first thing surely is to recognise our ignorance, our inadequacy; it looms tremendously large and threatening, and it seems impossible for us to face it. It immediately makes us feel small – but do not rebel against this feeling. When we feel small, let us realise that this is the first step towards solving the problem, for it is. We are going to accept something new, for we cannot solve any problem in quite the same way as before. (After Christ's baptism the Spirit drove Him into the wilderness to face new problems.) We therefore feel as a little child, we are receptive, open to new thoughts and ideas. (And do remember that it is the function of Christians to be open to new ideas; so often their one aim is to hold on to their faith, as if the important thing is not 'Glory be to the Father . . .' but 'as it was in the beginning, is now and ever shall be'.) Do not be frightened to feel very small. One of the most wonderful things in the whole Christian creed and the history of Christianity is the fact that our Lord in the Garden of Gethsemane could say 'Abba, Father'. The word Abba is what a very tiny child would say to his father, not a grown-up word at all - something more like 'Daddy'. If in that supreme moment of testing, Christ could be content to feel small, surely we should not refuse, in our lesser degree, a similar humiliation.

We are lying on the ground, dependent and accepting the love of God. It is very important to do that because so often the answer to our problem, whether disease in our bodies or anxiety in our minds is to have time to grow. We never seem to think that God needs time, and we need time. We have to wait upon God and wait for something to grow. So often people say, 'I am praying for strength' or courage or healing, and reckon this is a virtue. We have to be dependent on God and, for the time being, content for the strength of God to be made perfect in our weakness; first of all we must be weak and humbly accept our weakness, and be very quiet and humble in the presence of God, waiting for something new to grow. It is the only permanent answer to the problem – a new wisdom. So often one has to be content to be ignorant, or even blind. I remind myself and other people of the closing words of the ninth chapter of St John's Gospel, where our Lord pointed out that if only the Pharisees would accept their blindness, they would see – in a new way. We go through the cross of suffering, sometimes of shame, sometimes of weakness, physical or emotional or spiritual, and then we find that God, who raised Jesus Christ, is raising even us from our previous troubles and difficulties and giving us a new spiritual strength which was not there before. We can go out into the world and express the love of God and the power of the Spirit, but not unless we have been weak first. In our humble way we are simply expressing the whole life of Christ, and when we have a new difficulty, we should remember that we are going through the same spiritual experience as He went through. It is so wonderful to find how God creates a new picture in our mind when we become as a little child and receive something from God in the same way as our Lord did. He learned wisdom himself and grew into spiritual manhood, and we are able to face some of the real difficulties and problems of the world because we allow the Holy Spirit to lead and direct us in this kind of way.

To sum up: what is our problem and difficulty? We are going to be dependent, not afraid to be weak, learning to be as a little child; and we shall let a new picture grow inside us, so that we are gradually receiving the power and knowledge and wisdom that we need. We no longer have to go out in our own strength and power. It brings a glorious feeling that we can always draw upon this Life and Love within us. If only we can – in our lives just learn this inner guiding of the Spirit, we shall go out in the world to show in our own way (however partial and incomplete) the real pattern of life as God designed it. The world has lost its way, and the Christian Church has often been at fault in the practical application of its doctrines because we have not studied the working of our minds and bodies, as God designed them to work.

RELATIONSHIP

For, against, with

Ease of mind and body is considerably affected by our attitude to People. We may achieve relaxation on our own, but immediately we are with others, we feel disturbed, on edge, or at their mercy. Our relaxation seems to disappear, and we are a prey once more to waves, mild or acute, of unnecessary emotional feeling. It might almost be said that we are born first into the world of things, which we learn to have and hold and use. We live in this physical world and continue to live in it. We enjoy physical activity, its vitality and health. But there is another kingdom to be entered and enjoyed, the kingdom of people. Till we have entered it, we are left in the world outside, and feel empty and excluded from the heart of things. To enter it is to be born a second time, into the world that really matters.

There are only three possible attitudes to other people, which we can describe with the help of three useful little prepositions: 'for', 'against', 'with'.

We can exist *for* people. This is the attitude of service and well doing, which gives a motive for living. Surely this must be the right attitude, so most of us think, and yet there is a catch in it, a very serious catch which has proved the undoing of many. If we live for others and make our aim to be 'selfless' (as most good Christians are taught to do), then 'selfless' we shall become.

We shall find ourselves more and more weighed down with the burden of life. We feel that we are underneath everything and everybody, and everything and everybody are on top of us. We are likely to be plagued more and more with thoughts of guilt and inadequacy and, if our pursuit of 'selflessness' continues to its logical conclusion, we shall feel that death is very much better than life, and may be tempted to hasten its conclusion. The difficulty is simply this: that, for better or worse, we are a 'self' and, if we aim at the elimination of 'self', our subconscious mind interprets this to mean the dissolution of self in death.

Even if we avoid that difficulty, we are only too likely to fall into another. By being unselfish, we so often make it possible for someone else to be selfish. The married man or woman, for instance, whose aim is consistently unselfish, may be encouraging his or her partner to remain selfish. It is one thing to accept sacrifice, put up with hardship, or tolerate injustice, in a good cause, but it is well to make sure that our motives are above suspicion and that it is not sheer timidity which is the principal ingredient in our behaviour! Only too often Christians on a large scale have withdrawn from the struggle of life, abandoned their responsibilities and permitted control of a country or a civilisation to pass into the hands of wicked men merely because they were too 'unselfish' to make their influence felt.

The alternative preposition is 'against'. This is a far more common attitude than might be supposed. Many of us who think that we are 'for' a cause are in fact 'against' something else, as when we vote for a political party, not from conviction in their favour but because we are against their opponents. Many people cannot get on at all unless they are fighting somebody; it gives point to their lives and direction to their activities. They would be entirely lost without it. It is an unhealthy drug, this feeling of antagonism. Its worst effect is the feeling of superiority. We are 'on top of things', we are on top of ourselves, and we are on top of other people – and from every point of view that is an unhealthy position to be in. It is horribly close to being above all laws and regulations and exempt from the ordinary lot of man. Unfortunately, to maintain this attitude, we have to go higher and higher. Fortunately for us, nature usually succeeds in bringing us low, into depression, disease, misfortune, as the case may be: 'pride goes before a fall'. But we are only too apt to imagine that others have engineered our downfall. We see enemies on every side, and as we are against everyone, everyone in the end seems to be against us. The logical conclusion of maintaining the 'against' attitude is, therefore, a persecution complex, or worse.

'For' and 'against' are much the same, therefore, as 'under' and 'over'. Neither is a right attitude to life. In one we tend to be dominated by others, in the other we dominate them. Either attitude might be described as an attempt to enter the Kingdom of God in the wrong way. In the first we try to bribe our way into happiness, in the second we demand it with threats. Neither attitude can be anything but forced and unnatural. One spells inferiority, the other superiority.

True love is neither of these, for true love 'seeketh not her own'. True Love is simply 'with'. Only those can be 'with' who have shed their desire to have and to hold, and wish to be neither above nor beneath their fellow men. The way into God's

Kingdom of people is through the only door, the person of Christ. To establish the attitude of 'with' we must first be with Christ 'I call you no longer servants, but friends'. To be with – neither above nor beneath, but with – our fellow human beings is an attitude of trust and confidence, of relaxation, of freedom. To give up our attitudes of inferiority and superiority may not be easy, and we may be tempted to think, while we are doing it, that giving up these attitudes will leave nothing in their place, and that may be one of the reasons why we cling to them. But if we do cling to them we lose that freedom of the spirit, which is surely among the most precious gifts of God. A natural attitude, spontaneous, unforced, which is neither giving too much nor demanding too much, neither submissive nor overbearing, is the basis of spiritual freedom, and on this any temporary attitude can be superimposed. Thus we can be 'for' when it is right to be 'for', and 'against' when it is right to be 'against'. We need not be 'for' when it would be right to be 'against', or the other way round. We are not bound to be slaves and we are not bound to be tyrants; we are not fixed in either of those attitudes. We can be just ourselves.

Just ourselves

Most of us know what a tuning fork looks like: imagine a tuning fork, to give the note middle C, with a small magnet so arranged on either side of it, with a mechanism like that of an electric bell, so that, when the current is turned on, the vibration set up by the magnets will make the tuning fork sound its note. So far that is quite simple. Now imagine that, by varying the frequency of the impulses in the magnets, the tuning fork can be made to vibrate more rapidly, or more slowly, than normal; so that, while the current continues to flow, the tuning fork can be made to sound as sharp as C sharp, or as flat as B natural. The tuning fork is forced out of its natural key by forces exercised by the magnets.

That simple illustration will serve as a parable of what happens in the spiritual life. Throughout life, but particularly in early life, we are liable to be pulled out of our natural 'note' by people of powerful temperament who exercise an attraction over us of one kind or another. We may be tuned too high, or we may be pulled down below our natural level. One way or the other, it always makes us feel very guilty.

It cannot be emphasised too often or too strongly that God wants us to be ourselves. We are not being ourselves if we are living our lives, consciously or more often unconsciously, under the influence of someone else. Sometimes the situation is obvious enough, but sometimes it works in reverse. Here is a young woman, for example, who boasts that her life is her own and entirely free: she is bound to nobody and has no ties. Such an idea of 'freedom' should make us extremely suspicious. If we know the young woman well enough we shall see at once that she is fighting the spell of someone in the family circle, very likely her mother. She is 'anti-' everything which her mother stands for, and imagines that she has won her freedom.

But in practice she is controlled by her mother (in a reversed way) almost as much as though she was directly under her mother's thumb. Consciously she thinks that she is living her own life; but in the depths of her heart she is fighting 'mother' all the time. Very likely her inner life is doing its best to convey a warning message to her through her dreams; she probably has dreams in which she behaves very aggressively against some other woman. Outwardly she will tend to be afraid – of her own sex and regard all men old enough to be her father with exaggerated emotional feelings, while finding it hard to establish a permanent relationship with a man of her own age. Similar examples could be given in plenty.

Most of us, in our more honest moments, know quite well that we are swayed emotionally – attracted or repelled – against our better judgment by certain people in certain circumstances. Some people give us confidence, others deflate us; some upset us, others we give in to. We also realise, if we are being honest, that as the result of all this we are, as St James mercilessly describes it, 'driven by the wind and tossed'.

It is important in ordinary life, it is vital when one is trying to find physical health and nervous stability, to realise that God wants us to be ourselves. We cannot give ourselves to God as ourselves, if we are trying hard all the time to be someone else. God loves us first for what we are, not what we think we ought to be. So long as we are trying to be different, faith becomes a tremendous effort. We have to see through this illusion, and look at faith the other way round. Faith is an abiding in God, a resting in the divine life which is in us. By 'not resisting' the push and pull of the world, by just being passive to the emotional attractive force which certain people exercise over us, we learn to give the Spirit (within us) the first place in our lives. We are thus learning to live our own lives, instead of being at the mercy (emotionally) of other people. When that happens, we are no longer 'driven by the wind and tossed'.

More important, it makes 'empathy' possible. Our emotional attitude to other people is a form of primitive sympathy in which we feel very much what they are feeling. When someone has an accident for instance, we are liable to be so overwhelmed by feeling, that we are emotionally paralysed and rendered useless. But when we are more ourselves, we can use the feeling to become aware of their real need. We are not overwhelmed by the situation but challenged by it. In that way we become of use, to God and man.

CHAPTER FIVE

The
Renewal of
Trust

The first thing to remember, and one has to remind oneself of it constantly when one has been ill for a long time, is that we are made in the image of God, just as Christ is in the image of God; so His form, His nature, *is in us.*

Healing, therefore, is not something selfish or personal, but the release in us of the image of Christ, *which He is even more anxious to accomplish than we are.* God feels in us, and wants to feel our health, not our pain.

So our aim is to be 'fellow workers with God' in this (as in every other) matter. Faith and confidence are primarily 'sharing everything with God' so as to allow God complete entry into every part of our life – physical, emotional, intellectual, spiritual. We can do this if we abide or dwell in the Spirit.

God is Spirit, and God is everywhere – there is nowhere where God is not. So God is in us, and we rest in ourselves and find that we are resting in God. So we let ourselves go in order that the love of God in us (the indwelling Spirit of Christ) may be released in every part of us. 'He that dwelleth in love, dwelleth in God and God in him.' Christ promised His friends at the Last Supper that 'as the Father is in me and I am in the Father, so I will be in you and you in me'.

So we relax and enjoy the feeling of rest and the feeling that everything is becoming more natural. As stress and strain fade away, we have the feeling of becoming as a little child again, which, as Christ told us, is an essential preliminary to entering the Kingdom of Heaven.

Now all the difficulties will begin. Immediately we decide to give ourselves to the Spirit, we find ourselves in the wilderness, being tried by quite a number of devils. We do not resist evil;

we do what our Lord did, and let the thoughts and feelings come to us, for that is the way of healing. (It was the Spirit that drove Christ into the wilderness to accept these trials, which He did not resist or run away from.) Our part is simply to tell God exactly what we are feeling and thinking and what comes to us in these times of quiet and meditation. We shall find that, as the tension in our bodies decreases, so waves of every kind of feeling will creep up into our minds. If we accept them and give them to God and live the feelings in His Presence, we shall find His light appearing in the darkness. As each tension is broken, that particular tension will not come back, as it has come out of darkness into light. Whatever is healed in this way is healed for ever.

In this way we accept as adults many things which happened to us in childhood, of which we have no conscious memory at all. When we are experiencing extreme fear, for example, it is the sheer, utter terror of the tiny child, who cannot help himself in any way at all. We have to be the tiny child ourselves and feel that feeling all over again, accept it and give it to God, and it will do us no more damage. Or it may be that we shall find burning feelings of unfairness and injustice; these too must be brought to God, lived again in His sight and given to Him – as the Good Shepherd holds forth His hands to us and begs us to give Him all these burdens and fetters of our lives.

Another feeling that is almost certain to appear is a yearning desire to receive affection – very natural in a child but necessarily rather disturbing to an adult! This is a wonderful opportunity to give oneself completely to the Love of God and realise that God wants us to understand that the fullness of His Love is indeed given to each of us. I know many who have taken a new lease of life when they could realise that, however much God loves the rest of mankind, He also loves each one of us in a unique way. Not only does God believe in each one of us, but He also loves each one of us *for ourselves.*

This solves another problem that is often very baffling: if I am conscious that my parents did not love me as a child, (I have heard this so often), will this leave me spiritually and emotionally maimed for life? The answer is no – I can rest in the Love of God. When St John says in the first chapter of his Gospel: 'as many as received Him, to them gave He power' (or the opportunity) 'to become children of God, even to them that believe in His name, which were born, not of blood, nor of the will of the flesh, nor of the will of man, but of God', he means that the miracle of spiritual re-birth is the discovery within us of a much deeper source of life than the emotions and feelings that we derive from our parents. We are not limited by their love or lack of love, or the fact that we do not even know who our parents were, or whatever else may be the trouble. *Underneath all this* is the 'well of water springing up into everlasting life', and it is this flow of healing love that is natural to us – the other is a distortion.

We then begin to realise that, despite all appearances to the contrary, we have within us the Word, the indwelling light and life of which St John speaks. We can then let every thought and feeling be brought into harmony with these much deeper feelings.

Even thoughts of depression and despair, which many of us spend so much of our time in fighting and repelling, will yield up their secrets and turn into a source of good. If we accept depression and loneliness, we find that this will lead to a deeper realisation of our dependence on the power of the Spirit within us. If we accept failure and tell God quite frankly that we feel that we have failed, we shall draw closer to Him Who was the world's greatest failure, and, by being a failure with Him, we shall find a new spiritual vitality. Life will begin again, and we shall make the great discovery that St Paul made, that *nothing* can separate us from the Love of God which is in Christ Jesus our Lord.

For the Love of Christ is inside us, the Spirit of Christ is within us, all the time working through our infirmities (even when we do not know what to pray for or how to pray for it), and all the healing that we need is really there, if we are content to do nothing, and resist nothing, but simply start wherever we are, tell God exactly what we are feeling and thinking, and see what happens next.

For healing is a process; in most of us it needs time to grow. It grows when we are content to be weak, and make no effort to be strong. At first we shall feel hopelessly weak, that this weakness is going on forever, and that nothing will ever happen. But as we learn to *wait* upon God, and are not always trying to fill the gap in our lives by making great efforts of our own, we find that something is growing up inside us which is genuinely a new development, something which has not been felt fully before. At first we shall feel very naked, foolish, defenceless, exposed to life, and very tempted to go back on our good resolutions. But if we quietly persevere in trust, we shall feel the gentle stirrings of new life, the coming of new clarity and conviction, the diminution of illness, anxiety and pain. In this way the power of Christ, the strength of His image within us, is steadily gaining ground.

A prayer

In doubt and perplexity my heart shall be stayed upon Thy love; in weakness and self-distrust I will remember Thy presence in my heart. Thou wilt help me to trust when life goes wrong, and to believe when danger threatens and troubles are many, for Thou dost lead Thy flock like a shepherd, and through dark places we find the light. Whatever befalls me I accept it as food for my soul, knowing that I am enriched through suffering and strengthened by joy. In Thy strength I can learn both how to be abased and how to abound, for I rest in Thy wisdom and Thy will. In health or sickness, in failure and in success Thou wilt be my guide. Help me to accept the unknown without fear and the unexpected without dismay, that I may live my own life in Thy eternal presence, and enjoy it as Thy gift.

CHAPTER SIX

The
Relief
of Pain

Mrs X is in bed, in considerable pain. The trouble is arthritis and it has been coming on for many years. Every morning the disease seems to have gained fresh ground and it seems harder than before to make the movements that she did yesterday. She has learned a stoical heroism from her pain, is determined not to give in to the disease, and prays to God daily that if the disease cannot be taken away, she will be given the grace to bear it and be as little a burden as possible to those about her. There are times when she feels desperate, but in front of strangers at least she manages to keep a cheerful countenance. She is quietly grateful if no one will talk about the trouble. 'I never talk about myself,' she says, 'most people find life hard enough as it is, without adding my troubles to their own.' Her courage and fortitude are beyond all praise; all honour to her, and thanksgiving to God for the grace He has given her to bear suffering and pain. Can He rescue her still further from her disease? 'This woman whom Satan hath bound, lo these eighteen years . . .'

The problem is to let God into every part of one's life – physical, mental, spiritual. This is hard enough at any time but in a painful disease of long standing this is very difficult indeed. For that reason we need to pray so much more for our friends who are in this sad condition. They are never very far from depression and need all the support and encouragement that we can give them. The disease often starts in a period of spiritual and physical lowness or loss of vitality – at the end of a long period of strain, for example – and these depressed feelings are never far below the surface. That means that the sufferers are very lonely.

When we are lonely and in pain, it helps us most to draw near the Presence of Christ and remind ourselves that He suffered all pain. We can find true fellowship with Him when we realise that He feels in us: we are not alone in our suffering, because He is feeling with us and in us, and in the lives of all who are suffering, whatever it may be. There is a very big difference, first of all, between trying to 'get on top' of our own suffering (as most of us do) and trying to get underneath it, as He did. The easiest way to give Him our suffering and pain is to tell Him all about it, as frankly and trustingly as a child would. There is no room for pretence here; say exactly how frightful the pain is, and don't be afraid to get really angry and worked up about it! It may be right to bear pain silently as far as other human beings are concerned, but in the presence of God we must be absolutely honest and frank, or we are holding something back; and if we are holding back something we are not letting God into something, and His healing cannot work.

This point must be stressed, because, if anything is going to happen, it is supremely important that *everything* should be open to the love of Christ. Because so often we do not do this, we are both bad intercessors and continue to be ill ourselves. Yet it stands to reason that, if the love of Christ is not admitted everywhere, there are parts of ourselves that the love of Christ cannot entirely reach. One simply needs to be childishly honest about everything that one feels or thinks.

If Mrs X is doing this honestly, she will be very surprised at the amount of 'negative feelings' that come up into her mind. In plain language, she will find herself irritated, morose, disagreeable, and possibly worse than that. If she is again prepared to be honest, she will tell God exactly what she is feeling and thinking. Most people feel at this point that they must put all these thoughts out of their minds, as it is wrong to think these things; that they must ask God's forgiveness for thinking them, and dismiss them as soon as possible. That is why they go on suffering from arthritis.

We must give to God all our feelings of shame or guilt in these matters, and continue to be honest, for that is the only way that progress can be made. If we feel irritated with somebody, it is much better to tell God exactly what we are feeling; the more we let ourselves go in His presence, and pour out our hearts before Him, the more relief we shall feel.

Now here is the surprising and unexpected result: the more we can get rid of our negative and aggressive feelings in this way, *the less pain we shall feel*. The reason is simple: all pain in the body is amplified out of all proportion to its original cause by the mind itself, which seizes the opportunity thus given it of releasing its bruised feelings. I knew someone once who had intense pain in her neck. Medical examination revealed the beginnings of osteoarthritis. Whenever she saw me, the pain became intense. So I explained to her that she was intensely annoyed with me underneath, while remaining open and friendly on the surface; if she would tell God honestly and frankly what she was really thinking about me, the pain would go – which it did.

The rule is really quite simple. Our inner feelings must have an outlet. There are many occasions when we cannot say what we are really feeling and thinking, for any number of reasons. The feelings that are thus denied expression find their way out through any other feelings that are in the mind – we are terribly tired, hopelessly bored, unduly excited, or in great pain, as the case may be. We cannot be frank with man, so we must be recklessly honest with God. In that way we find true relief.

We *shall* find it. Every wave of pain is a wave of negative life, life that is going the wrong way, down into ourselves, adding itself to the tension and discomfort of the body. But this process *can* be reversed. We can bring these hidden feelings to God and share them with Him, thus finding deeper feelings and fuller life. The healing of pain can thus become the way of spiritual discovery. We may fail more times than we care to number; but if we accept failure honestly, we learn through it quicker than any other way. We do not worry over failure, but quietly leave the whole life open to God. God is finding His way through my pain; through it I am finding God's way to God.

For meditation

Christ told us 'not to resist evil'. I am not fighting my pain, but accepting it as part of the process of healing. I know that Life is within me, and that God's healing is finding the way. I am learning the meaning of my weakness and letting my body teach me the truth that God wishes me to know. I have not used wisely the life of God within me; I have been unfair to myself, to others, to God. Now I have gone back a step, that I may go forward again along a better road. I will therefore rest and let my strength be renewed. I will accept my fears and not be frightened of fear, and let them lead me to a deeper trust. I will accept my anger, and find a new use for my energy. My real wishes and longings I will give to God who guides me from within my heart, and I will pray that they may be satisfied in any way that helps others besides myself. Through this pain I can enter into the suffering of others and find that my loneliness vanishes in my prayers.

A prayer

Thou who through Thy suffering upon the Cross didst enter into the joy of Thy Resurrection, I open my heart and my whole life to Thee. I know that Thy love is indeed within me, and is helping to bear my pain. For this purpose Thou didst suffer, that Thou mightest find the way into the hearts of all who suffer, and add Thy strength to theirs. I thank Thee every day for Thy love within my heart, and pray that it may daily become a larger room and fill the whole mansion of my mind. In my heart I bring to Thee every trouble and every difficulty that lies upon me. Thy wisdom will guide my mind, Thy love will strengthen my desire, Thy life will heal my body. Henceforth I am no longer desolate, but united in spirit with all who enjoy Thy love. Through pain and suffering I will find the gateway to new life. Remember I pray Thee, the poverty of my understanding, and show me by Thy light within me the way that Thy love has already chosen for me.

CHAPTER SEVEN

Imagination

To most of us imagination is something of a nuisance, because we have no idea how to use it. How easy it is to imagine, for example, that one is ill! I know when I am driving a car alone, how easy it is to imagine that the engine is making the wrong sort of noise! It is the same with the body; when we are alone and have too much time to think about ourselves, little aches and pains can be magnified out of all reason. This is particularly the case when we become over-sensitive to disease. We realise that disease can be passed from one person to another by physical infection; we are only just beginning to realise how well the way is prepared for it by emotional contagion.

The trouble is that mere words have such a hold over us. Their influence is almost mesmeric. The very names of diseases cause waves of anxiety to flow over us. Cancer, heart disease, insanity – what appalling pictures they conjure up! There is good reason for saying that suggestion is the worst part of them.

Years ago in America, a man of 65 was knocked down and killed by a car. His wife was heartbroken; her husband had never had a day's illness – and then to go like that! The post-mortem revealed that his heart was in a poor condition, there was something very wrong with his liver and his kidneys and he had a TB lung; four diseases, any of which might have killed him, but he did not know and lost no sleep in consequence.

Out of a hundred people suffering from heart trouble, investigation showed that 98 had been exposed emotionally to the disease. They had watched someone suffer from it, usually a member of their own household. But only 45 of them could have inherited any supposed tendency to the disease. The others had all had the suggestion planted deeply in their sub-conscious minds.

Heredity is another bogey of this kind. About 73 per cent of normal people are said to have an insane relative or ancestor; the proportion in the case of the insane is said to be only 78 per cent. Here again, emotional contagion is probably more important than inheritance.

If you find out tomorrow that you are suffering from cancer, what are you going to do? Relax completely, to relieve this congested area of the body. This prevents the growth from getting an abnormal share of the body's resources. Cancer means that the ordinary functioning of nerve and gland has been thrown out of gear. If more of us learned to relax, the peril of cancer would be much diminished. By refusing to allow such a bogey to mesmerise us, much of its power to hurt us is destroyed.

The force of suggestion is particularly strong when we are exposed to it in childhood. We then accept disease as part of the ordinary course of things and this idea of it is deeply implanted in the imagination. Disease is bound to happen, and the remembrance of another's sufferings intensifies this suggestion. Thinking about disease in this way is a pernicious habit. It is not really difficult to break, once one has made up one's mind to break it. The Christian glories in health as the gift of God and expects to be healthy. We are bound as Christians to give no encouragement at all to those gloomy people who glory in disease in all its forms.

Much the same applies to our little habit of expecting the worst! Some people are naturally cautious, but many others pride themselves on a caution which is carried to a harmful extreme. If you are always expecting the worst, pull yourself up sharply and point out to your own mind that you are really wishing the worst! You would hardly wish the worst to happen to other people, so why wish it on yourself. I am quite sure that this attitude of mind in parents, for instance, is a constant source of disease in children. If such thoughts are in one's mind they are bound to take effect somewhere. In most of us they proceed from an underlying feeling of loneliness, the feeling that we are cut off from God and man. We will hardly admit that we are inwardly envious of others, but that is just about what it amounts to.

These are some of the obvious handicaps of the wrong sort of imagination. One could mention plenty more. Some of us cross our bridges before we come to them. Others of us can cross bridges in the most optimistic way if they are two or three bridges ahead of the one we are immediately coming to. Others again fail to see the bridge at all, because they are spellbound by the width of the river or the depth of the gorge they are expected to cross.

In fact, before we can come to the right use of the imagination, we have often to recognise that we have many bad habits to get rid of first. If one has some habit to break, the very first thing to do is to think of it as a trivial habit which is no longer necessary.

One can de-hypnotise oneself – excuse the expression – by repeating quietly to oneself during the day, 'I need not think like that any more'. Gradually we come to realise that the particular habit is largely an artificial way of thinking. We have very little need then to break the habit. As we cease to accept it, we are starving it of energy and it quickly dies away.

Much as we might remove a wart by tying a bit of cotton round it, so that the blood can no longer flow to it, so in the same way these foolish and unnecessary blemishes in our spiritual life can be starved of their vitality and left to die a natural death.

All this is obvious when one has thought about it, but not obvious until one has. And one mentions these things particularly because one meets too many Christians who adopt the wrong attitude to problems of this kind. It is no use praying in an agonised sort of way, day after day, to get over a bad habit of thought or action. One is merely thinking more and more about it and driving the habit deeper in. One should pray to be released from it and believe that one is being released from it and devote the energy thus saved to other purposes! Habits are an immense saving of energy, and the building up of health is immensely assisted by forming good habits of thought and action.

We do this quite naturally as we meditate and say our prayers. Every time we do this, we grow in the way God has for us. Christ is being formed in us all the time. It is a natural process which proceeds unconsciously. It is a growth in freedom, as we lose wrong habits of mind; a growth in health, in energy, in staying power, as we lose foolish conflicts which sap our reserve of strength; it is also a growth in imagination, as we begin to see possibilities in place of disaster. As we grow in God's grace, our imaginations grow more active. The imagination without God can only see disaster; it is filled with thoughts of everything gloomy, sorrowful and unpleasant, and sees pictures of this everywhere. But the imagination which begins to be God-inspired, sees disaster as the opportunity of providing something better. Very often things have to break down before they can improve. Disease can often be turned into a grand opportunity for acquiring fresh health. Many of life's apparent disasters can profitably be treated in the same way.

As the imagination begins to refuse to accept apparent disaster as the end of everything, God is able to take us a stage further so that we see life more and more as a series of opportunities which we can turn to spiritual profit. Most people are surprised to find that the Saints of history were nearly all very practical people, with abundant commonsense. They did not always start in that way, but under the training of God that gift was developed in them as they learned to use their imagination.

Perhaps it will help us to realise that the imagination is our gift of creative ingenuity, always producing something new. It is quite easy to let our imaginations use us; we become slaves to it and are mastered by it. The imagination is a wonderful servant but a shocking bad master. If we do not use our imagination it will use us; it will produce wonderful, new and ingenious worries, fears, and anxieties of all kinds. If that is what we like, our imagination will do its best for us and gladly help in any way it can! But if we give our imagination to God, it becomes the means by which God's wisdom and grace can reach us and solve our problems, so that we can meet life's troubles with ingenuity and resource – which is the reason God gave us imagination in the first place.

CHAPTER EIGHT

Fatigue

Fifty years ago, a great Indian scientist the late Sir Jagadis Bose, studied the effect of fatigue in plants. There is an Indian variety of mimosa (*m. pudica)* which closes up like an umbrella if you touch it. Bose was fascinated by this plant and investigated it scientifically. He found that the basic phenomenon is common to all plant life, though very few plants have developed a method of showing it. For instance, he took a freshly-cut section of any common vegetable, such as the carrot or the cabbage, placed one end in a tiny vice and gave the free end a pinch or a tweak. This set up an electrical impulse in the stalk of the plant, exactly comparable to the impulse which would run up the nerve of one's arm if anyone touched it, and proved that the cabbage possesses not only life but something more – a capacity for registering sensation.

Bose made some further discoveries about this capacity. The cabbage could register separate tweaks or pinches without difficulty, but when they were repeated quickly, the second or third impulse followed the preceding one too closely for the plant to recover itself between one impulse and the next. This meant that the strength of the second impulse was added to the first, the third to the second, and so on. When this happened, the cabbage obviously 'felt' far more deeply and spent much more energy in doing so. After a number of such impulses, the cabbage suddenly got tired and registered no further sensation. It 'passed out' as we would say, and had to have a long rest before it returned to normal and began to register again as before. Under the influence of a drop of alcohol it at first registered more strongly, but passed out rather sooner and took longer to recover. A drop of something poisonous at first acted as a stimulant, but rapidly became too much for it. In fact, whatever there is in a cabbage works in the same kind of way as the human nervous system, and the picture of the cabbage may help us to understand one or two points about the behaviour of our own nerves which would otherwise seem puzzling.

Suppose that we are listening to a continuous loud noise, for example. The noise rapidly becomes unbearable, and we do our best to shut it out. This does not mean that the noise has in fact become louder. The noise remains the same; what has happened is that one noise being very quickly added to the next, the total effect very soon becomes intolerable, because of this 'summation' effect inside our own nervous system. Exactly the same happens whenever there is a repeated stimulus of a constant, monotonous kind. Merely to walk down the same street every day is depressing for most of us, and even the things we enjoy pall after a time if there is no variation in them. Things we do not enjoy, rapidly 'get on our nerves' and the analogy of the cabbage helps us to see why. Of course, individuals vary enormously in this respect. To some of us a certain amount of routine is absolutely necessary and our tolerance of repetition is fairly high (and also our tolerance of pain, for our nervous system is physically tougher and more resistant). But when our bodies are tired and our nervous systems equally tired, then the phenomenon of the mounting effect becomes more obvious.

One point that need scarcely be mentioned is the importance of relaxation here. A short rest, if only for a moment, helps to break the feeling of mounting tension, and a number of short breaks in a long or monotonous task can be very refreshing. The mere act of breaking off from what we are doing gives the nervous system a brief opportunity to recover. Many of us would get on far better if we worked with great intensity for shorter periods, with breaks in between. (Sir Winston Churchill would serve as a good example of this system.)

There is one point about fatigue which is of particular importance. It can be very distressing to see someone convalescing after a physical or nervous breakdown. Every now and then he believes that he is at last very much better and tells you that he is now really getting on top of things. Whenever I have this said to me, I make the sufferer rest immediately. One knows from experience that in a very short time this feeling of well-being will suddenly disintegrate, and the sufferer will collapse in great weariness and probably also utter despair. This is extremely puzzling to those who experience it, unless they realise what has happened. These feelings of mild elation are not evidence of recovered strength but of mounting fatigue. We have no way of knowing what the cabbage feels when it experiences its mounting sensations, but we know what we feel. It is a sense of being above other people, above the law, or a law unto ourselves. We feel as if we could go on and on at what we are doing, as though we have some invisible flywheel inside us which will never come to a stop, and that we are suddenly filled with something which feels like 'eternal life'! All that is actually happening is that we are getting more and more keyed up. Excitement is a dangerous drug for all of us, and this particular excitement a more insidious danger than most. So far from giving us new life, it is taking more out of us than we imagine – and all nature's debts have to be paid in the end. The end-effect is the same collapse that the cabbage experiences, and we fall into a horrible pit. There are naturally other factors in depression besides extreme fatigue, but those who are prone to depression should take precautions against over-fatigue. Directly we feel that slightly exalted feeling coming over us, we should take notice and have a break in what we are doing, however short. Unfortunately, when this effect sets in, it is extremely difficult to give up what we are doing and rest. We have nervous breakdowns just because we find it so difficult to stop. We already have a premonition of the disaster which looms ahead, and that forces us to continue. We are liable to an awful swing between elation and depression, from which only complete rest will rescue us. But once we recognise the difference between a real feeling of returning health and this spurious feeling of elation, which is the danger sign of fatigue, then we shall be able to cut out our effort before the danger point is reached.

For those who are suffering from any illness, whatever its nature, and for those who are suffering from overstrain, it is of the utmost importance that they should only do half what they feel they can do, and that they should rest immediately they feel the first signs of this false confidence coming over them. And for all of us it remains true that excitement is a dangerous drug, which stimulates us to begin with but exhausts rather quickly. Any form of interest is excellent, as this is food for mind and body. The way to health is to eschew excitement and find a new interest in each returning day; for most of us, anything that lessens monotony lifts a load from mind and body. If we have to walk down the same street every day, let our curiosity stimulate us to discover some fresh thing about it every time we pass. When we are on the lookout for new and rewarding experiences we shall begin to find them. But if we want to see we must first look! Monotony is largely a habit of mind, to which the greater part of the world has been trained. It is a habit which cannot be broken, but which may well be given up! Even if I am lying in bed for many hours of a long day, I can ask the constant help of the Spirit to avoid it becoming monotonous. In prayer for others I can learn to be spiritually creative. Life is full of richness and variety if we let it disclose itself.

Teach me, my God and King,
In all things Thee to see.

A prayer

O Lord, who didst know both weariness of the flesh and heaviness of the soul, I make my prayer to Thee. Help me to rest and abide in Thy presence throughout the day. Keep me from the heights of life, that I may be preserved from its depths. Give me the true enjoyment, that I may make the most of life, without effort or anxiety. Give me the wonder and wisdom of a child, that I may find new marvels on every side and new interests in the life around me. Enable me to take people as I find them, and to accept them for what they are. Prompt my mind continually with Thy wisdom, that I may avoid the mistakes of the past and see the way before me more clearly. Save me from false fears, and give me friends who will understand.

CHAPTER NINE

Nervous
Indigestion

Excitement of any kind can upset the digestive tract and under the stress of emotion we produce annoying and distressing symptoms. We may just feel sickness and loss of appetite, or some kind of cramping pain, or acute diarrhoea. But we go to the doctor who decides that this is mainly 'nerves'. We are not quite sure then, whether to feel comforted that the trouble is apparently not mortal, or annoyed that he should think us 'neurotic'. But we are not alone in this. Anyone can suffer from gastric symptoms under strain; it is all a matter of degree. Uneasiness or fear can close the opening at the lower end of the stomach, or reverse the peristalsis or muscular movement by which food is carried through the digestive tract. Excitement can produce flatulence, bad breath, 'heartburn', or the flare-up of an organic disorder, such as a gastric ulcer, in which case the continuing emotion causes the gastric juices to go on flowing long after there is no food left to digest. Much of course depends on the physical sensitivity or irritability of one's nervous system. There are people who can go to sleep while having a tooth drilled; I must admit that I am not one of them! At the other end of the scale are those unfortunates who in any excitement are prone to blushing, a rapid pulse, excessive sweating, trembling, frequent urination, feelings of faintness and abdominal symptoms.

Much depends on one's constitution, much on the degree of one's fatigue, but the sensitive will always be sensitive. Shelley complained that after an illness, blades of grass and boughs of trees seemed painfully distinct. Flaubert described his sensitivity as sharper than a razor's edge; the creaking of a door, a face he saw in the street, or an absurd statement, set his heart off and completely upset him. Many people after an illness like influenza can feel their heart going, or listen to the throbbing of the artery near the inner ear, or can feel the contractions of little muscles in the skin. When there is a 'lowering of the mental threshold' small disturbances in the body are proportionately magnified. But these problems can be felt more cruelly than organic disease, and patients who suffer from them often beg their doctors to find something physically the matter – hence much unnecessary treatment, physical and surgical, which merely focuses attention on the organ still further. This is a pity as it becomes an object of affection, about which we naturally feel over-emotional, and tend to respond to the whims of this organ with the same concern as the lover has for the caprices of his beloved! In fact, this often has a history. If mother, for instance, is over-anxious about our heart or digestion, so that her affection for us has been canalised along this route, the feeling of any deep emotion will throw this organ out of gear. It is often a source of 'nerves playing tricks'; violent waves of feeling, which would normally work themselves off in activity, are projected inwards and throw the inner mechanism of the body out of balance, but we do not recognise the unconscious factors in the disturbance.

I read an instructive instance of this in an American book the other day. A woman of 50 went to her doctor, feeling very depressed. She was very disappointed that he 'did not find anything wrong with her'. There was in fact plenty that was wrong, but none of it was causing her symptoms. She had *some* symptoms of thyroid trouble, but the surgeon had removed part of the gland a year before, without relieving the situation. She had stones in her kidneys, and two in her gall bladder, but neither of these physical facts was responsible for any symptoms. She had a little trouble in her uterus but it was not getting any worse, and no one wanted to disturb it. She had high blood pressure, but its effects were insignificant. She was in the menopause but hormones had not helped her. She had trouble in the bladder, but it might easily get worse if anyone began to treat it. Her real trouble, which no medical treatment could touch, was simply that after years of her negative feeling and thinking, her husband had tired of her constant complaining and was finding consolation elsewhere.

It is a comforting and reassuring thought that the human body can put up with so much without getting into real difficulties. Nowadays we are much too conscious of the possibilities of disease. Perhaps the advertisements are partly to blame. Undoubtedly we are at the mercy of a great deal of sheer nonsense. We have made too much of 'poisons in the system' or the effects of 'too much acid' as a cause of arthritis, for example; the biochemist assures us that if the blood becomes even slightly acid, death would follow pretty quickly! In the same way we have worried far too much about the possible effects of constipation. What does the damage is not the effects of constipation but the worry it gives us! Even the headache which attacks some people when they are constipated is more likely to be due to the sense of guilt and rebellion which still hangs round this particular mechanism of the body, a carry-over from nursery days when it was the occasion of many battles. In many people this region of the body is deeply disturbed by emotional memories.

In fact feelings of guilt are at the root of many of our troubles. It is because we feel so deeply that we ought to be like other people that we feel these handicaps so keenly. One ought almost to ask, as Adler used to do when a child was brought before him, 'Who is this child measuring himself against?' It is obvious that of two brothers, the one of frail physical endowment is not merely going to feel inferior as he would do in any case, but is going to feel all the worse by comparison with his very athletic and physically well equipped rival. In childhood all the admiration went to the physically capable child, and no one thought to solve the problem of the frailer child by finding something at which he could excel. We have to learn to use our resources as best we can. The obvious example is Darwin, who for 40 years could only work three hours a day. Even a quiet evening with friends would knock him out emotionally and leave him sleepless, shivering and vomiting for several days. Thomas Huxley once wrote: 'I have not, now, nervous energy enough for stomach and brain both, and if I work the latter, not even the fresh breezes of this place will keep the former in order'. We simply have to accept ourselves and live within our means, till strength returns.

This helps us to accept and adjust ourselves to our emotional vulnerability. A very young child regards the whole world as part of itself. Mother's feelings are the child's feelings, as it cannot separate itself from her. If it is detached too violently from mother, it goes on being attached to mother underneath, without realising the fact. This means that we feel everything that is going on in the world around us to an enhanced degree, like Shelley and Flaubert. Nothing happens and we are not affected! It is impossible to detach ourselves from anything that happens around us, and feel our feelings as our own: we are always being swamped by someone else's. We think we can shut these things out of our minds, but if we are made that way (or rather, if we have been made that way) we shall do better to accept the situation. Otherwise we shall be at the mercy of those unconscious forces, a prey to 'little storms of some kind streaming out over the autonomic nerves to the heart, the blood vessels, the digestive tracts, the kidneys, and the several structures of the skin'. The sufferer may then feel any of the symptoms we have mentioned already with a few more that we have passed over, such as urticaria, stopping up of the nasal passages, salivation, or fear of impending disaster! Just nerves!

The only answer to these problems is the long way round of learning to relax and so to detach oneself from other people's feelings, as a prelude to finding out what sort of person one really is. There is no substitute for that. But it is a great help if we can realise that when we feel one of these nervous storms coming on, we are being at the mercy of someone else's feelings (or what we think their feelings will be!); then we are one stage nearer freedom. The surplus of emotion means that we are identifying ourselves with someone else. Who is that person? It may be a particular person or a group of people, but at least they are not God and we must keep them out of heaven! In some way or other we are making an idol of them, and they need to be de-idolised. At the moment we are conforming to someone else's pattern, and we need to ask Adler's question, who am I measuring myself against here? Then let the old enemy go with thankfulness!

CHAPTER TEN

The Riches of Middle Life

The first buoyancy of youth carries us along through the early trials and disappointments of life, giving us the conviction that our luck will change, that something better is always round the corner, that if we continue to do our best, virtue and hard work will eventually bring their own reward. But as life lengthens, we lose this early optimism. If we successfully achieve what we aim at, we find that our ambition no longer satisfies us; it has become a dead-sea fruit, fair to look at but disappointing to consume. If we fail to gain our hopes, life becomes stale and unprofitable, seeming to lead nowhere. Our first vigour has begun to wane, and physical vitality can no longer be squandered happily, without thought for the morrow. What will take its place?

When the average expectation of life hardly exceeded 40 years, the problems of the second half of life scarcely mattered. If I am to die young in any case, 'gather ye rosebuds while ye may' may well seem the right policy. But now that the normal expectation of life, artificially assisted by modern medicine, has nearly doubled, the problems of the second half of life, which hardly troubled our forefathers are now of enormous importance. What is not generally realised (though Jung pointed it out 30 years ago) is that human nature has a second flowering in middle life. This begins when the first flush of vitality is exhausted, between 30 and 40 perhaps; it is the growth – the emergence from the depths of one's being – of the other side of what we are.

At this stage a man finds his latent femininity emerging. Up till then he has needed some woman – mother or wife – to carry his other nature for him and draw out its qualities; but now they begin to make their presence felt on their own. The woman similarly discovers the growth of her masculine side, which has previously needed a man or a male environment to evoke it, but now comes into its own. Both men and women find this new prospect intimidating. If we have never learned to use and handle our deeper feelings, we have no technique for solving the problems which this new development is presenting to us. These strange new sensations seem to undermine the very idea of ourselves. A man who has previously prided himself on his masculinity feels himself overwhelmed by an unexplained weakness; he feels unmanned, no longer himself, pursued by feelings that are quite foreign to him, which he describes as 'driving him mad'. On the woman's side the difficulties are well known and quite needlessly dreaded. Yet the physical changes in the woman only mirror what is happening in her inner life. Left to itself, the body can manage these changes very well. But so many terrifying legends surround this phase of life that few women approach it without a sense of panic. The very phrase 'change of life' suggests a disastrous upheaval, and loss of personality. If we called it 'fulfilment of life', we should be much nearer the truth and approach it much more happily.

We should look at the matter from the spiritual point of view. God's plan is simply this. In the first half of life he needs us as men and women, either sex representing (as we might say) half of His own nature. We are strongly developed in one direction or the other to start with, as God intends that most of us should take part in His design for the creation of further human beings. But when the time for that has gone by, then the other half of life is developed and enriched in its turn. This is not a change to be dreaded, but a fulfilment to be expected and welcomed. We should gladly cooperate with God in bringing it about, and look forward with keen interest to what is going to happen.

Many changes have to take place, but we need not be afraid of them. What is fatal, is to resist the process. If we co-operate with it and realise that it is a natural development we shall find that it carries us along gradually, and is nothing to be afraid of. But there are two difficulties which must be faced. The first is the change in my idea of myself. I have formed a picture of myself that has guided my life for many years. It is this picture which now seems to be in danger. I am no longer 'myself'. What we have to realise is that this picture has never been completely true – not what I am, but what I thought I was. I am now being brought to see the many flaws in the old picture, and this unwelcome discovery is precipitating a crisis. I can no longer paper over the cracks, and pretend that they do not exist. Can I love myself sufficiently to accept these facts? If I love myself unwisely, like a spoiled and pampered child, or if I hate myself and believe almost anything bad of myself, I shall cling to the old picture of myself and dread any change. But if I love myself wisely, I shall regard this new development as a great step forward. Up till now we have always been at the mercy of these flaws in ourselves. Part of the real joy of the second half of life is the opportunity which it gives us of getting our life in order. We can see not only where, but why, we have gone wrong. Repentance consists in both seeing this and using the new insight constructively. We cannot undo the past, but we can redeem it by making use of its lessons. Even the saddest and most crippling experiences can be used by God when we seek His understanding and commit ourselves to His care. The reward of suffering is to find how many doors it opens in the lives of others; and that is a great reward indeed.

The second, and for the religious mind the greatest difficulty is to give up our ideals. There comes a time in life, usually about now, when it is vitally necessary to our spiritual development that we give our ideals back to God and ask that we may be shown where they are wrong. We are apt to assume without thinking that ideals are always right. Unfortunately that is unlikely to be true. Our ideals tend to become a sort of spiritual bottleneck through which the main stream of life cannot pass. The fears that we are afflicted with, correspond to ideals that are too narrow. Life is dammed up within us and cannot get through. Our forward look in life is that part of the self which reaches forward in advance of the rest of us; the star which we see and follow. But this ideal has to grow and develop as the years go on. If it fails to grow, we are left barren and impoverished; that is why we feel 'dry'.

Of this deeper development of the soul there is an illuminating instance in the New Testament. We read of St Paul's conversion, and we rather tend to imagine that he had no need to grow spiritually after that first wonderful experience. But when we look at his later letters and compare them with his earlier ones, we can see that there has been a deepening of his spiritual life in this particular direction. When he writes to his friends at Thessalonica, he hardly seems the same man as the writer of those wonderful last letters to his friends at Philippi and Ephesus.

We can see how much his tenderer side has grown and developed in the meantime. It shows the extent to which he has been led to accept his femininity. There is further evidence of this. In his earlier writing there is a tendency to be afraid of women and to disparage the sex relationship. But towards the close of his life he seems to see deeper into things, and we actually find him using the analogy of husband and wife, the closest relationship that we know, to express the relationship of Christ to His Church! This is surprising when we think of his earlier letters. Has he found a way of reconciling his masculine aggressiveness with his inner, rather submerged, tenderness? Perhaps that reconciliation first began when God told him: 'My strength is made perfect in your weakness'.

Through trusting and abiding in the love of God we grow more wise and though physical vitality may diminish and work may have to be given up, it remains true that 'nothing can separate us from the love of God which is in Christ Jesus our Lord'. We all know men and women who to the end of their days are trusted, consulted and used of God in the service of their fellow human beings because they remain lively channels of His grace. They have found the spiritual treasure within them; you may be sure that they travelled by this road.

CHAPTER ELEVEN

Praying for the Sick

To be desperately ill is to be desperately lonely. When health collapses, faith collapses too. All the hidden doubts and fears, which are kept at bay in normal health, rush into a mind left defenceless by the loss of its usual interests. A dreadful fatigue and lassitude come over mind and body. It seems horribly unlikely to the sufferer that he will get better. Anything he has ever read about disease comes into his mind. No doubt 'they' are concealing the truth from him. It seems impossible to wrestle with the problem any longer. Certainly, no one can be blamed for losing faith when they are ill.

This is the point when they need our help. When the four friends brought the man sick of the palsy into the presence of Christ, it was *their* faith which Christ noticed. The early Church prayed regularly for sick people, and its members held services at the sick bed. Can you not imagine, if you were desperately ill, what a comfort and encouragement it would be to know that not only your friends, but some complete strangers as well, were taking time and trouble to remember you in their prayers? 'Bear ye one another's burdens, and so fulfil the law of Christ.'

There is a lovely instance of this in the New Testament. In one of the last letters which he wrote to his friends, St Paul assures them that everything will turn out all right for him through your supplication and supply of the Spirit of Christ' (Phil 1:19). The fact that they are praying for him in Philippi means that he is supported and comforted in Rome. He realises that they are indeed supplying 'the Spirit of Christ'. The warmth and sympathy of his words seem to reflect the gratitude which he is feeling. He writes to Corinth in the same way (II Cor1:11) 'You must help us by prayer, so that many will give thanks on

our behalf for the blessing granted us in answer to many prayers.'
But there is another occasion in the New Testament when friends
did not do what was needed – 'couldest thou not watch one
hour?' The sick often feel as lonely as Christ did.

In prayer we are putting ourselves at the side of the sick person
and supplying 'the Spirit of Christ'. Let us be clear, first of all,
that we are not attempting in any way to alter the will of God.
Many people still have this curious idea about prayer at the back
of their minds. We are not asking God to do something which
He does not want to do. The will of God is not the edict of a
capricious dictator, who may or may not be disposed to listen
to our anxious requests. As the Prayer Book says, He is 'more
willing to hear than we to pray and art wont to give more than
we desire or deserve'. It is a little misleading to think about God's
will, for the word 'will' means wish or desire, and when we think
of the will of God, we should think at once of the overwhelming
love and compassion which we find in the nature of Christ. Love
went out from Him to heal the sick: no one appealed to that
love in vain. The will of the Father is yearning desire to help
His suffering children. Why then do we need to pray? Because,
until we pray, we cannot receive: Our asking is an
acknowledgment of our need for help. Frequently the sick are
not helped until *they* ask, if they hold back from asking because
of a feeling that they do not want to be helped. We are already
receiving all the help which God can give us *as things are*. The
acknowledgment of our need, and perhaps of our fault, is the
opening out of our lives to a yet deeper inflowing of the love
of God. It is only asking, that makes this possible: it is only
receiving, that accepts it and enables it to come true. It is not

what God does *to* us, but what He does *through* us (as Agnes Sandford has pointed out). Through our prayers we are offering ourselves to the will of God, that yearning compassion of Christ, that love which is so much more than our love. In so far as we have discovered that deeper love in ourselves, we can be the means of disclosing it in others.

The essence of prayer, then, is that we are moved with compassion ourselves for sick people. In that we share in the divine compassion, we are sharing also in the 'will' (or yearning) of God on their behalf. Compassion enables us to reach out to the person we are praying for. But compassion by itself is not enough: we must be receiving for that person the love and vitality of the Spirit.

Sickness is, therefore, a challenge to us personally. If we are afraid of illness ourselves, the help that we can give is limited. Fear cripples our faith and undermines our courage. The first step towards helping others must be to free our minds of the fears which so easily attack them. Only when we are free from fear ourselves, can we come to the rescue of others, without danger. Otherwise, we shall be defeated by their troubles, and superimpose them on our own. When we begin to see the answer to our own problems, we can use the same resources for others. We take the sick person into our own prayers, and believe that what has helped us, is also helping him. Physically, our bodies are separate; Spiritually, our minds are never far apart, and we can never pray the open prayer of faith ourselves without praying it for others as well. To wish others well is an unconscious prayer; to do it consciously in God's presence is to bring in a new spiritual world to redress the balance of the natural one. We are taking part in God's process of setting the world free from the tyranny of fear, disease and pain. We are 'fellow-workers with God', working as members (or limbs) of the Body of Christ. By our spiritual activity, we are realising the presence of God in the hearts of the people we are praying for.

There are many ways of doing this, and no one right way. Prayer for the sick should never be a strain, and it is most important that we should find the way that comes easiest and most naturally to us. The way that I find most helpful myself is to pray to the Holy Spirit *in* the sick person. The life of God is in them, or they would not be alive at all. But the life of God is in them incompletely: they have lost 'life', or they would not have fallen ill. Two things have happened. First, the 'life' has receded within them, leaving them 'lifeless', and then it has burst out through a wrong channel. Think of cancer, for example. For some reason which we do not understand, though we suspect that stress comes into it, certain cells of the body start multiplying furiously, at the rate at which they multiply normally in the body of an unborn child. There is a parallel happening in what we call a nervous breakdown. Certain aspects of our inner life assert themselves violently and irresponsibly, in defiance of our wishes. In either case, it seems that when life is denied, it is liable to burst out in us in a form of disease.

We can think of the life of God as being in the sick person, but leaking out in the wrong way or taking the wrong path. We are praying, therefore, that this life will reassert itself in the right way. At the moment he (or she) is less than a complete personality. We are asking the Holy Spirit (the Spirit of wholeness) to come in the fullness of personal life – as a trinity of love, light and life – and restore the wholeness of the person that we are praying for. We are not trying to impose something on the sufferer from outside, but asking that he may have the full realisation of the fullness of the Spirit *inside*.

Just as it is a help to ourselves to offer our cares and anxieties to God and find a new link with God by doing so, it is equally a help to the sick person if we make a similar offering on his behalf of all his troubles and difficulties. We are praying that he will be enabled to admit God into every aspect of his life, with new spiritual vision, new understanding, new trust, new freedom and new strength, on every plane, spiritual, mental, emotional and physical. We are praying that the love of Christ may flow in his spiritual veins and that his body may indeed be a temple of the Holy Spirit. We could hardly sum it up better than in the words of St Paul – 'that (God) may grant you to be strengthened with might through His Spirit in the inner man, and that Christ may dwell in your hearts by faith; that you, being rooted and grounded in love, may have power to comprehend with all the saints what is the breadth and length and height and depth, and to know the love of Christ which surpasses knowledge, that you may be filled with all the fullness of God'.

CHAPTER TWELVE

The Meaning of Prayer

'Whatever you pray and ask for, believe that you receive them, and you shall have them' (St Mark 11:24). The word 'receive' is in a past tense, which is not quite translatable in English. The Revised Version reads 'believe that ye have received them', but that goes a little too far. 'Believe that you always receive them' probably conveys the sense as well as any translation can do. It is the complete certainty that all prayer is always answered, that is the basis of Christ's teaching (St John 11:42, 43).

Prayer is not cajoling an unwilling deity into giving us something which he does not want to give or which will do us harm if we have it. There is no need for 'vain repetitions'; prayer is not the repetition of a magical formula. Our Father knows what things we need before we ask Him. No human father worthy of the name would give his son something harmful when he needed food; no friend worthy of the name would fail to answer a friend's request for food, however inconvenient the time and circumstances might happen to be. But the initiative must come from our side; no one can receive without asking or find without searching. 'Ask and ye shall receive, that your joy may be full.'

I never find it possible to read the various passages from the Gospels which give us Christ's teaching about prayer, without realising what a fantastic parody of His teaching our own ideas of prayer have been. Our picture of God is always of the unwilling deity who is most unlikely to give good gifts to his children – the pagan picture that Christ tried so hard to replace with reality. We are afraid of our prayers, as we are afraid of real living in whatever form we find it. We are afraid to take risks, afraid of putting our faith to the test. We are afraid of being disappointed, we have been disappointed before, and feel we shall be disappointed again.

Our main difficulty is this: we do not realise that *all* our prayers are being answered. Not only the prayers which we succeed in uttering, but all the other wishes of our minds are, in fact, unconscious prayers. If we can imagine all our wishes becoming prayers, we can understand fairly easily why prayer is so often apparently unanswered. We simply do not know what we really want. It is not just that our surface wishes are conflicting; there is an even more serious conflict in our deeper minds.

That is why Christ warns us so carefully that we must forgive our enemies before we make our petitions. 'When you stand to pray, forgive if you have aught against any.' Unfortunately, the significance of this emphatic advice, which comes so closely after the earlier statement about prayer, is usually missed. Many earnest and devout Christians, believing sincerely in 'the prayer of asking', have come to terrible grief because they have overlooked or neglected the equally essential advice about forgiveness. 'Agree with thine adversary quickly whilst thou art in the way with him'; failure to do this means that all sorts of hates and fears begin to make their presence felt in the mind, and the harder we pray, the more active these become. How indeed could it be otherwise? Prayer is a great force, energising the whole life; and prayer will energise all those parts of our life that we do not like, and the resulting disharmony is bound to get worse, until we learn from experience that Christ's advice cannot be disregarded.

Thus it often happens that the first result of our prayers for healing is that the symptoms of fear and disease are aggravated. That is why I prefer, as a rule, to help the sufferer to understand that faith is trust and health is an abiding or resting in God. 'Remission', whether of sin or disease, is a 'letting go', and no sin or disease can be remitted unless the sufferer really and truly desires to let it go and learn, through the experience, whatever the Spirit of Christ would have him learn. As sin, fear and disease have this in common, that they are all based on a negative attitude towards some one person or group of people, the forgiveness of others is an essential part of our growth in health and insight.

In all cases of nervous suffering, this element of injured feelings goes so deep that the 'prayer of asking' can hardly be used at all. If we pray for healing, all the 'devils' within us seem to start fighting together. So it is usually wise not to pray this prayer at all, but to substitute for it the prayer for truth – 'seek, and ye shall find'. It is the truth that makes us free. By resting and 'letting go' we give our disorderly feelings every chance to sort themselves out, which indeed they are always trying to do; unless they were, we should have no hope at all!

The truth is that we are made in the image of Christ, and this design of God is continually asserting itself in our lives. As St Paul pointed out, the Spirit within us is praying all the time, although we do not realise it. Our deepest desires and aspirations, in other words, come from God, and we can bring them closer to God by making them conscious in our prayers. The deepening of our faith consists mainly in finding out what we honestly and sincerely want.

We shall grasp this more clearly if we realise that every anxiety in our minds is a conflict between two desires. I want something to happen at the same time as I do not want it to happen. Am

I afraid that I shall not get well? Here is an obvious instance of the natural desire to get well being negatived by a strong, and unadmitted, desire not to get well, which appears therefore as a doubt, a fear that our prayer will not be answered. Is it surprising therefore that both prayers are answered, that we get better and worse alternately, or that improvement is followed by a relapse?

And if we analyse that fear, that desire not to get well, we shall find a fear of life itself; we shall be lonely, perhaps, or we shall lose our privileged position, or we shall be exposed to difficulties that we do not know how to cope with. It is a curious paradox that we tend to seek safety in disease when we are afraid of something happening to us, something that has perhaps happened to us before in our early childhood, though we cannot remember it. In some way we were hurt, and that hurt has remained as a festering spiritual sore. Corresponding to that sore, we shall find that we have great difficulties with certain types or groups of people who stand for us now in the place of whoever hurt us formerly. If we pray for them and for their good, we shall be solving our spiritual problem. If we pray that the Spirit of Christ may be formed in us and in them, we cannot pray a better prayer than that.

As we grow in love towards God, so we find these practical problems working themselves out. In this way we gain outlets for our spiritual life. Or, if you prefer to put it more accurately, our spiritual life gains outlets through us; because, through all our spiritual wanderings and struggles, it is the Spirit that prays for and through our infirmities and is always guiding us towards the goal which God has for us, and not the goal which we have for ourselves.

So the work of God in the world becomes more and more the release in us of the divine Love. Fuller life and fuller prayer develop hand in hand. Part of our work for God is the bringing of others to Him to share in the same love. Laubach in his book on Prayer suggests that we think of it in this way; it is our way of *helping God.* Usually we pray to God to ask Him to do something for our friend. But we are surely on the wrong track! God is much more ready to help our friend than we are to ask His help. But between Him and our friend there may be a wall, which God has not yet been able to get round. Our friend's link with God is too small for the fullness of His life to pass into that sufferer. But that friend's link with us is a further way into his heart. If we are 'with' him in spirit, and if we open that link with him to the Spirit within us, we are opening up a further channel by which the Love of God can help our friend. Not only are we helping our friend, but we are helping God too. To that end we must consecrate ourselves, as Christ said that He consecrated Himself, and offer ourselves gladly to Him for the growth of His work

'In the most noble part of the soul, the domain of our spiritual powers, we are constituted in the form of a living and eternal mirror of God; we bear in it the imprint of His eternal image and no other image can enter there. . . . This image is found essentially and personally in all men; each man possesses it whole and entire and all men together possess no more of it than does each one. In this way we are all one, united in our eternal image which is the image of God, and the source in us of all our life and our coming into existence. Our created essence and our life are joined to it immediately as to their eternal cause. Yet our created being does not become God any more than the image of God becomes a creature.'

John Ruysbroeck (1293-1381) The Mirror of Eternal Salvation

CHAPTER THIRTEEN

The Meaning of Death

Death is not a catastrophe, but a change of energy by which we emerge from one condition of life to another. It is not so much an event as a process. We start to die as soon as we begin to live, because dying is part of living. The difference between me and a stone is that the stone neither lives nor dies. Living is a taking in of energy and dying is giving it out. Unless our bodies are continually dying and giving out, there would be no room to take in, no room for fresh development. Strictly speaking, as soon as we cease to die, we cease to renew ourselves and the whole process begins to slow down and finally comes to a stop.

Dying is thus an essential part of living, and that is how we should think of it. Before we were born, we were alive, but incompletely alive. We certainly had no conception what our future was going to be. We emerged from the confined space in which we first grew, into a larger existence, with greater and more developed capacities. When this stage of life draws to its close, we emerge into something greater still; this time discarding the physical envelope of the body which has served us well or ill, so that we can burst out into a new and more glorious existence in which our latent spiritual powers come into their own. That happened uniquely and completely in the case of Christ. It happens less completely but none the less wonderfully, to you and me.

Christ did not say that we *shall* have eternal life, if we believe in Him, but that we *have* it. When we use our spiritual powers in prayer for others or for the healing of the sick, for example, we are already growing spiritually and enjoying something of the life that will finally be ours. Here, we can only know in part and love in part; then, we shall know, love and see, more fully. Our life here is a continual growing in the capacity to love and to understand (or in the failure to love and to understand). These powers will be extended still further in the life to come. We cannot imagine a future life without a great development of the gifts that we value most. We shall keep and develop further, our individual identity, and must be recognisable as separate individuals. We shall have some method, simpler and more direct than we possess now, of taking energy in and giving it out. Our 'bodies', not being physical, will be less bound by the physical laws of this existence. We shall be able to give love and life to a greater degree. Is it mere coincidence and nothing more, that all the miracles that we find so difficult to accept, in the life of Christ, show this further life already emerging in Him? The feeding of the five thousand, for instance, is utterly incomprehensible, unless we think of it as the changing of one state of energy into another, in a way that belongs to the next life rather than to this one. The giving of love in the healing miracles, the exemption from physical forces in walking on the water; the transfiguration, in which a state of spiritual energy seemed already discernible in His present life; the final bursting out of all His energy when His physical body dissolved and disappeared; are all these examples of a new state of spiritual life manifesting itself through the veil of this one? If He believed that His followers could possess 'eternal life' here and now, He must have believed it even more of Himself.

Throughout His life and teaching He takes the fact of 'eternal life' for granted. 'In my Father's House are many mansions: *if it were not so* I would have told you.' He would have been the first to tell us if these things were not true. 'It is expedient for you that I go away.' Why? In order that He could give them His love in a new and spiritual manner. 'They shall be as angels in heaven . ...' 'Fear not them who kill the body, and after that there is no more that they can do.' 'The Spirit quickeneth, the flesh profiteth nothing' and so on. His whole estimate of life is based on the belief that this existence is a temporary phenomenon, not to be compared with what is to follow.

Can we have the same faith? In the first half of life we are frightened of death for now it would be untimely. Our powers are undeveloped, our knowledge slight. God's design is to equip us to live and develop our capacities as far as possible within the framework of life as He has arranged it. We rightly avoid death if we possibly can. But in the second half of life, this consideration no longer applies with equal force, for we are no longer needed so much. Our children have grown up and are not now dependent on us, rather the reverse. We should, therefore, prepare for death, not as a disaster and not as an event which will necessarily be painful, but as a natural event which will, in fact, be a re-birth into a new and greater existence. But many of us are held back by the same fear of death which up till now has been an asset. Our inner mind tries to free us of this fear by forcing it up into our minds at every opportunity. So long as we refuse to face and accept it, it may well seem a sad and frightening prospect. But like any other fear, it represents a secret desire. We are now beginning to want death and to look forward to it. So we turn this fear into a prayer and face it in the presence of God. At first, the fear may increase, but soon it begins to lose its sting. Spiritually, we are already 'dead' or 'alive'

– whichever way we look at it. We are already accepting the new love and freedom that we feel deep down within our hearts, and we can give ourselves to that, more and more. A much deeper peace and conviction begin to flow into our lives. We begin to feel that we are getting past death, and are feeling our way into the unseen. This does not mean that we get lost in dreamland; on the contrary, life seems to have a greater reality. We learn to rely on that reality and begin to understand that we *have* eternal life. We are part of something much larger than we are, and are in communion with reality greater than ourselves. We do not lose our individuality; but our individual life is both more defined and yet shares in, as it draws upon a much wider whole.

At one of the supreme moments in the Communion service, when the congregation joins 'with angels and archangels and the whole company of heaven' in a burst of thanksgiving to the Father, it seemed to the early Church that we who are here, and they who are there, are in fact all together 'in heavenly places'. Together we share in the spiritual gifts of God's presence. It was a tremendous strength to them, and it should equally be strength to us. St Paul could speak of the Church as a 'colony of heaven', an outpost on earth of what already existed in the life to come. We should share the same faith, and believe that the love and prayers of those who have gone before us are given freely to us, as ours are to them. If we had any idea of the new kind of life which they lead, we should cease to be sorry for them when they die. We should be sorry for ourselves rather than for them, as we should be if anyone we knew was going a long way away for a long time; but we should know that we were going to be reunited in the end. So for them, at least, we can be glad.

A prayer

'Blessed are all Thy saints, O God and King, who have travelled over the tempestuous sea of this mortal life, and have made the harbour of peace and felicity. Watch over us who are still in our dangerous voyage; and remember such as lie exposed to the rough storms of troubles and temptations. Frail is our vessel, and the ocean is wide; but as in Thy mercy Thou hast set our course, so steer the vessel of our life toward the everlasting shore of peace, and bring us at length to the quiet haven of our heart's desire, where Thou, O our God, art blessed, and livest and reignest for ever and ever:'
(St Augustine)

CHAPTER FOURTEEN

Being –
Saving –
Healing –

Basic words in the Bible

1. The being of God

To be: The key to understanding God. 'Be' is a very dynamic word in Hebrew, much stronger than in English. In translating the Old Testament we have to use a variety of verbs where Hebrew uses 'be'; eg 'a famine *arose* in the land', when Hebrew says simply (and correctly) 'famine is'.

'To be' means much more than 'to exist'; 'to be' is 'to have an effect'. This is the meaning of Moses' vision of the burning bush. In the kind of waking dream which has so often opened the eyes of inspired religious people, Moses saw 'being' as generating the fire of life in living things; 'the bush was burning, but it was not consumed' (Ex 3:2).

Chemistry caught up with Moses at the end of the 18th century, when Lavoisier summed it up in a memorable phrase: 'life is a candle flame'. Every cell of the body is a miniature furnace; as in the burning bush, the fire burns, but does not consume.

But over and above this Moses hears 'the name' of God – what describes God is 'being': I AM THAT I AM. The *living* God is intensely personal. Bishop Ian Ramsey used to say that the word *God* and the word *I* are intimately linked; if I do not believe in 'God', I cannot fully believe in 'I', and if I do not believe in 'I', I shall find it hard to believe in 'God'.

What of the tense? In Hebrew, tense does not imply *time* past, present, or future. There are only two tenses, *perfect* (complete) and *imperfect* (incomplete); 'I AM' also conveys 'I have always been' and 'I shall always be'. When the last writer in the Bible wants to translate 'I AM' into Greek, he is reduced to the clumsy phrase 'the Most High, who was, and is, and is to come'; the Hebrew 'I AM' is both more realistic, more emphatic, and more concise.

Christ uses the Hebrew idiom: 'My Father worketh hitherto and I work' (John 5:17), meaning that 'my Father has been working all the time and will go on working'. In Christ the impact of God is described as abundant (better, overflowing) life; 'as the Father has life in himself, so he has given the Son to have life in himself' (John 5:26). So Christ can take to himself the full, tremendous meaning of the words 'I am' (John, 8:24, etc).

Hebrew therefore brings out much better than English the full impact of 'being' – the living God. To say that God is, means far more than saying 'God exists'. 'The Lord be with you' means nothing in English (or Latin, or Greek) but means everything in Hebrew – the full impact of the God cleanse you, comfort you, energise you, heal you. 'I will be with you' is a promise of power.

Save, heal: Save and heal are the same word in the Semitic languages. 'Save' is said to mean 'to enlarge; to make a man capable of dealing with his enemies'. The verb is reserved in Hebrew for the activity of God. It can mean forgiveness and material help, as well as physical healing. (From this root come the proper names Joshua (ie Jesus), Isaiah and Hosea). God's *being* is always effective.

Love: God's *'being'* is effective as love (not 'mercy', a tragic mistranslation). Love is rather too sentimental a translation of the Hebrew 'Hesed', for Hebrew is always very concrete and practical. 'Hesed' describes the attitude of a good father, who never lets his children down and whose anger is the hot anger of love, never the cold anger of hatred. 'In overflowing wrath for a moment I hid my face from you, but with comforting love I will have compassion on you' (Isaiah 54:8,10). Hosea realised this; when his wife ran away and took the children with her, he found that he still loved her, in spite of everything and God's love must be greater than Hosea's (Hosea 11:3-4, 8-9). This is the kind of thinking about God that Christ so often used; 'if you being evil know how to give good gifts to your children ...' (Matt 7:9-11).

To sum up, 'being' in Christ is limitless love. Real love cannot accept any limit (or it ceases to be real love). Christ touched the leper, entertained the publican, healed the madman, comforted the woman by the well, so that they were enabled to be 'people of God'. Christ was expressing 'I AM' in the fullest way – 'the fullness of God bodily' (Col 2:9). How then, do we accept 'life' of God?

2. Man's response to 'being'

Trust: The Hebrew word (bata<u>h</u>) comes more than 40 times in the Psalms suggesting 'firm support such as the ground gives to the man who lies on it' (H Wheeler Robinson). Trust is first and foremost a state of rest, we rest that our thoughts can be renewed (Ps 4:8, 116:7; Is 30:15). It is the attitude of openness and receptivity in which the living God can work; as Christ put it, 'fear not, only trust'. 'The man who trusts' (wrote Martin Buber) 'does not possess the power of God; rather, the power possesses him, if and when he has given himself to it and is given it.'

Believe: A favourite word of Isaiah, probably from a root

which means 'upright' and so gathers to itself the word and spiritual meaning of uprightness - being open, honest, true to oneself, and so on, 'an Israelite indeed, in whom there is no guile'. The root gives us our word 'amen'.

God is trustworthy because God never changes, being true to himself. But trust must be an exchange of confidence; as Buber translates Is 7:9, 'if you will not trust, you will not be entrusted'.

Buber described trust and belief as the two poles of faith – the passive *receptiveness* which builds up into the active *steadfastness* which enables a man, under God, to stand on his own feet. Hab 2:4 sums it up; 'he whose soul is not upright in him, shall fail, but the just shall be known by his faith (or faithfulness) ... the arrogant man shall not abide. His greed is as wide as Sheol, like death he never has enough.'

Repent: The ordinary Hebrew verb (su<u>b</u>) for 'turn'. It is a key word in Ezekiel, for instance; 'if a wicked man turns away from sins ... he shall live, he shall not die' (Ez 18:21 etc). Jeremiah puts it more positively: 'if you return, I will restore you, and you shall stand before me ... They shall turn to you, but you shall not turn to them ... For I am with you, to save and deliver you, says the Lord; I will deliver you out of the hands of the wicked, and redeem you from the grasp of the ruthless.' (Jer 15:19, 21).

Turn - and trust: Christ's message ('repent and believe') means turning away from everything unreliable and turning to reality, trusting in the ultimate reality - God. This is a redirection of life, which will demand forgiveness or 'remission of sins'.

Forgiveness: Not just God's forgiveness. The new principle that Christ brings in here is mutual forgiveness, 'how often shall I forgive my brother – seven times? No, seventy times seven!' God is always forgiving, but forgiveness, to be experienced, must be passed on. 'Whenever you stand in prayer, forgive if you have aught against any'; 'forgive our debts, as we forgive our debtors'. Are we willing to *release* the people who have annoyed us? (If not we are obsessed by them).

The story of the 'defaulting manager' makes this clear. The owner of the estate returned unexpectedly and asked to see the accounts. The defaulter begs for time to pay, but then demanded (with appropriate threats) money from a junior colleague. The bite in the story is the size of the two sums of money. The underling had borrowed £20 or so; the manager had stolen about £2 million. In other words, our debt to God is infinite; what others owe us is trifling by comparison.

Release: The new principle of forgiveness means the annulment of debts; it means 'expiation'. Christ comes to work through the world's problems, and calling us all to share in the 'cross' – take our part in bearing the penalties of human sin, not retaliating in kind (an eye for an eye, a tooth for a tooth, a slap for a slap) but bringing good out of evil in any way we can. Christ calls himself 'a ransom for many' – a substitute victim for the world's wrongdoing, and warns his followers that they will be 'victimised' in the same sort of way. (Resist not evil – do not answer evil with evil's weapons). The 'release of debts' (remission of sins) means profit increase for the kingdom of God.

There are 'laws' which govern this new growth.

3. How do we come to understand 'constant love'?

Law (Torah): Originally an instinctive understanding of the laws of God's creation (later debased into a legal system). For the original inspiration see (eg) Ps19; the writer looks up at the night sky and marvels at the order of the heavens and the silence speaks to him (as the 'still small voice' or the 'whisper of the great silence' did to Elijah on the mountain top). In the second half of the psalm he marvels that this same order (divine law) is working inside himself:

The law of the Lord is perfect, reviving the soul;

the testimony of the Lord is sure, making wise the simple ...

Let the words of my mouth and the meditation of my heart be acceptable in thy sight, O Lord, my rock and my redeemer.

Wisdom: Solomon asked for the gift of wisdom; in Prov 8:22-31 'wisdom' is almost the imagination of God, guiding the design of God's creation from the very beginning. Christ goes back to this original idea of law (wisdom) as the unalterable expression of God's constant, unchanging love – heaven and earth would collapse if 'law' were abrogated or undone (Matt 5:18, Luke 16:17). Christ's own words proceed from this inner 'Torah'; 'heaven and earth wilt pass away but my words will not pass away'.

This inner direction enables a man to 'walk in truth' (Ps 86:11). The opposite of wisdom is nothingness (vanity) and instability which leaves a man out of control, like a ship without a rudder (Eph 4:14, James, 1:6, 3:2-5). Wisdom demands sincerity, and the acid test of sincerity is put simply in the Sermon on the Mount; in prayer, fasting and almsgiving, if none but God knew what I am doing, would I still do it?

New law: The Sermon on the Mount is based on the Hebrew word 'turn' (repent): Life must be reinterpreted and redirected in three ways. (i) Turn to God; loving God with all one's resources (the first commandment) means offering to God all one's defects as well as all one's strength. But this in turn demands – (ii) Turn to your neighbour; 'love thy neighbour' (Luke 19:19), the only place in the OT (according to M Buber) when love takes the dative case – love to thy neighbour. It is less important to feel emotionally inclined towards one's neighbour than to pay attention to his needs. (If the surgeon is taking out my appendix, I don't want him to love me, I do hope that he is paying attention to me). The natural corollary is; (iii) Turn to your enemy; we can all 'love those who love us'; the difficult task is to turn to one's enemy and risk his scorn, his refusal to respond, or even his active hostility.

The point that Christ is making is based on the 'being' of God. Because the Father is true to himself (with complete Hesed) he 'loves his enemies' and is turned towards them – thus he gives us sunshine and rain impartially to enemies and friends. As St James puts it (James 1:17) 'with him is no variableness, neither shadow cast by turning.'

We are never outside the light (and sunshine) of God – 'the Lord make his face to shine upon you.'

This is the real meaning of 'deny thyself', it is a question of abandoning ourselves – 'self (is) everything to which a man is attached' (M Buber). We experience 'a new self' when we 'come to ourselves' (like the Prodigal son), and make a new relationship with other people.

4. The effects of 'being'

Kingdom of God: 'the Lord reigns' (Ps 93:1, etc). As we should put it nowadays, everything is under control.

(a) It is the answer to his question 'what rules me?' If I am dominated by one instinct more than any other, I make an idol out of that instinct – aggression (Mars), sex (Venus), drink or drugs (Bacchus), and so on. Add to these greed (Mammon);'honour', 'prestige' etc all describing slavery to a set of impulses which I follow but cannot control.

(b) God is not concerned with things as they are, but things as they might become (not a static state of affairs but dynamic growth and change). God does not so much 'rule' as 'overrule' – he is always bringing good out of evil, order out of chaos, healing out of disease. Man is 'enlarged' through trust, which opens out fresh possibilities which must be asked for, looked for, opened up.

(c) God's 'overruling' can only be fully effective through people who trust and respond to his being – led by the 'messiah' whom God has anointed as leader (Hebrew, Messiah; Greek, Christos; English, anointed). All these represent 'judgement', or God intervening.

(d) God's intervention is the coming of a new age, through the healing of human ills:

'The well do not need the doctor, the sick need him.

I am not calling the righteous but sinners to turn and trust' (Luke 5:31-32)

God is becoming effective in a new way, which goes beyond law and wisdom: 'the return of the quenched Spirit'. The Spirit had been damped down by human sin (was the current belief);

now Spirit is released and 'adding' to the law and the prophets. The effect is expressed in a series of vivid phrases in a two-beat rhythm (a passage of poetry in the original Aramaic):

Blind see

lame walk

lepers cleansed

deaf hear

dead get up

the poor get the message

5. Acknowledging the spirit

Blessing, thanksgiving: At every meal the Father of the family offered the loaf of bread to the Father, thus recognising that bread is bread from heaven, for every good gift comes from above. The loaf was then broken and shared with everyone present. Every Jewish child had this object lesson of the meaning of faith - hallowing the name of God and sharing out the divine blessings. 'Blessed be God ...' is the normal beginning of prayer (many examples in the epistles).

Prayer: Personal 'thanksgiving', receiving the Being of God, who is Abba, Father (the most intimate of all words for God). If God is completely reliable, then child-like trust, with the openness characteristic of the 'natural' (ie undamaged) child (note that 'child*like*' is not the same as 'child*ish*'), is the birth of new understanding (turn and become as a little child, Matt 18:3-4). The basic virtues of the open life (open to God and man) are the virtues of the healthy child – intense curiosity, the certainty of being listened to, and a persistence that will not be denied.

In St John's Gospel (c 6) this becomes 'feeding' upon God – to do the will of him who sent me and to accomplish his work. Soon this 'feeding' will replace the Temple and its sacrifices. Feeding on God through Christ is the 'new covenant' (foretold in Jer 31:31), when all God's people will have open access to the Holy Spirit; 'peace I leave with you, my peace I give unto you; not as the world giveth (ie meanly, grudgingly) give I unto you'.

Peace: Shalom (the second half of Jeru*salem*, surviving in the Arabic greeting 'salaam') is not the negative condition of absence of conflict but the emergence of effective order out of chaos, because 'God is working everything together for good'. This demands trust: 'seek the Kingdom of God and this way of being right, and all the rest will be given you'. (This is not absence of foresight, but freedom from care.) It expresses especially the Hebrew idea of 'covenant' – a divine/human contract in which we bear one another's burdens and share good things and bad.

In Christ: St Paul's favourite phrase for Christians praying together and working together; he asks the Philippians (2:5) to behave during the rest of the week as they do when they are together 'in Christ' on Sunday. Together they form 'the Body', the different members (ie limbs) working together, with their different gifts, under the guidance of Christ as the Head.

In St John's Gospel Christ expresses this by using the word 'one' in the neuter gender. As Christ is '*one thing*' with the Father and the Father with him, so Christ will be *one thing* with his friends and his friends *one thing* with one another. He uses the old Jewish symbol of the vine and its branches to represent the same idea.

The Word: The writer of the Epistle to the Hebrews (1:1-4), St Paul (Col 1:15-20, 2:9, Eph 1:9, etc); St John (1:1-18) all use the idea of 'wisdom' to express what they believe about Christ. He is the reason for the creation, the pattern of the creation, and its basic formula – Christ gives meaning to, and makes sense of, human history – it all leads up to him (Teilhard de Chardin has written eloquently on this theme). The Word became 'entabernacled' in human flesh (John 1:14) because the whole presence of God is in them.

Body/temple: In the new age it will no longer be necessary to worship God on a mountain top (John 4:21) because the time is coming when the Father will be worshipped anywhere in sincerity and truth. The 'presence' (Shekinah) is not confined to the Holy of Holies in the Temple at Jerusalem; it rests upon all men of sincerity and truth but especially in the person of Christ, whose body is the (true) 'temple'. His enemies can destroy his body, but he will build this particular temple again in three days.

Son of man: Christ uses this phrase as it is used in the Book of David (c 7) to describe 'the saints' presented to the 'Ancient of Days'. Christ thought of all who accepted him as being 'one' with him and part of his body/temple/self. Son of Man is therefore a description of himself as incorporating all who are his, presented (through him) to the Father.

Death: Not regarded by (eg) St Paul as the snuffing out of a candle. Death is a state of minimal life through which we pass through to complete life. 'Dying' is being reduced to this minimum (II Cor 1:8-11); St Paul says that this 'crushing experience' convinced him of the 'transcendent power' (4:7) – the same resurrecting power which had raised Christ from the grave is raising up St Paul all the time; we are being crushed and reduced to nothingness all the time, through the impact of the world, but because we are suffering in the same sort of way as Christ did, so we are being raised up in the same way that he was (Rom 6:1-11). This experience of the 'transcendent power' is a foretaste of the Spirit, which will be freely given in the life to come.

CHAPTER FIFTEEN

Seeing
and
Believing

Some thoughts on
science and religion

1. The inside and outside of experience

Science looks at life from outside; religion approaches it from inside. The two viewpoints are complementary; neither is complete in itself, and both are needed for full understanding. A simple illustration will make this clear.

When I look at *you*, I see a face, the outside appearance of another human being, and this is the frontier between us which I can cross in one of two ways. The scientific approach is to look further and deeper. The radiologist, for instance, can pass x-rays through your physical system and take a look at your bones or the working of your digestion, and the chemist can analyse the elements that have contributed to the making of you as a physical organism and disclose that you are mainly water and a few chemical salts. This is the kind of information which can be obtained by looking at you from outside. How far is this the 'real you'?

We can take this point a stage further. When the dentist x-rays your aching tooth, he can detect that its condition is not what it should be. The physicist can measure the strength of the impulse, electrical in character, that is travelling up the pain nerve to your brain. He might (or might not) succeed in comforting you in your distress by pointing out the trifling nature of the disturbance about which you are making such a fuss – a few thousandths of a volt, or less; not enough to cause the faintest flicker in any electrical apparatus which we use for domestic purposes, but to you, or to me in a similar situation, it is still a very, very unpleasant experience.

Once again the point is quite simple. The dentist and the physicist are looking at this experience from outside. How are they to know what it feels like? They may, of course, have had toothache themselves; if they have, then they know what it feels like. But there is nothing in the x-ray or the physiological experiment which, by itself, can give the slightest inkling of what this inner experience is like.

Put like that, the point is simple enough, but the underlying principle remains true however complicated we make the example. The neurologist, to go still further, has ways and means of exploring the brain by measuring the 'brain waves' of the waking or sleeping subject, or by inserting electrodes into the brain itself to find out what movements this will initiate or what kind of sensation it may induce. In this way he can ferret out the centres which control memory or vision, sleep or pleasure or fear, but whatever he does, he is still only discovering where a particular kind of experience is physically located. By itself this does not contribute anything at all to his understanding of what the experience *feels like*. In other words, he is still exploring you from outside. No knowledge that comes through the eye can, in the nature of things, give any other kind of information. It must be an approach from outside, and the approach from outside can take life to pieces and show how it fits together, but it cannot by itself disclose what you and I are like, or what it feels like to be a human being. I only know what it feels like because I feel as well as see.

I could make the same point again in this way. Suppose that some scientist existed who was an absolute scientist and nothing more. He would look at everything objectively; which is another way of saying that he would look at everything with his eye and his eye alone. To him the bursting of a hydrogen bomb would simply be a displacement of atoms, an extraordinarily interesting release of energy, leading to the immediate carbonising of a multitude of organisms which had previously been listed as plant, animal or human. This is the only picture which his eye, as eye, can give him.

No scientist is an absolute scientist or anything approaching it – very much the opposite in fact. We can begin to make a guess at what a mind of this kind would be like because it so happens that a few human beings develop a kind of mental disease in which what they see with their eyes becomes completely detached from any kind of feeling. They are (if you like to call it that) completely objective, rather like a young child who dismembers a fly because he has never thought that the fly might feel the effects of this operation. 'Objectively' a man can commit murder without registering the fact that he is inducing any sort of suffering in his victim. This is so abnormal that we take its abnormality for granted. But why? After all, it is only the objective attitude pushed to its logical conclusion. One of the nightmares of our time is to fear that the nuclear bomb might well fall into the hands of some 'objective' paranoiac who would look at the world in just this way.

In practice, of course, we are never 'objective' in this way. We supplement 'knowledge' by feeling. By itself knowledge carries no meaning. Meaning is contributed by our personal reaction to what we come to know, and feeling is there first, before knowledge, and we never feel in isolation. Real feeling, or the fullest expression of feeling, is only liberated in the company of others when something sparks across the gap that separates one human being from another and 'takes us out of ourselves'.

2. The growth of individual personality

I feel myself when I feel something outside myself. As a child I raced around feeling the sun on my cheeks, the fresh air in my nostrils, the solid earth beneath my feet. This was heavenly. I also felt the full warmth of human approval (for no one enjoys showing-off so much as a young child) and occasionally disapproval. In one way or another I was in touch; even my naughtiness made certain that someone would pay attention to me.

This was all part of the process of growing up, of discovering myself through contact with other people. It began at birth, when I still felt as part of my mother, though physically separate from her. I felt her feelings as my own, even the feelings which she would have preferred not to acknowledge or recognise. Gradually I became more aware of my own powers, by contrast with hers. Then at a later stage I went on to discover the possibilities of 'me' with a whole series of people, starting with my father, on whom I 'projected' various aspects of my character. Parents (after all) cannot be good at everything, and the child finds older children and other adults to help it become aware of the full range of its possibilities. The process is always the same. I develop a hero-worship for some older person, and feel what (I imagine) he must be feeling. This quality grows in myself by imitation, and I begin to try it out for myself. In turn I develop qualities from mother, father, older brothers and sisters, and so on. My richness depends in the first place on the richness of my contacts. Later, when I begin to feel mature, I start projecting on to the opposite sex, so that the feminine can supplement the masculine. In every way by being in touch with others I become more aware of myself as a real being.

This applies just as much to our negative qualities; we take a step forward when we realize this. Whatever is stunted and repressed by my inner fear can only be released and begin to grow when I find someone who can carry my fear without being afraid of it. Because he (or she) knows what fear is (not the same as looking at a toothache only from the outside!), I can trust and discover myself in that other person, and by treading the road which he has already travelled, I can recover my nerve and begin to grow again. In this way a nervous breakdown can be a blessing in disguise. Untangling the knots in which I am enmeshed means that normal growth in self-awareness can be resumed.

As we grow older we no longer develop so fast, but the process is the same. Each stage is a letting go of the past and a reaching out to a future that can only be partly known.

Marriage fails, for instance, if the partners are not progressively extending their experience. The man who ceases to grow becomes identified with his profession - or his picture of himself whatever his work may be; so often his epitaph could run 'died at 48 retired at 65'. As one learns to live in spite of people, as well as because of them, one finds to one's surprise that it is one's enemies that help one most. There is a religious truth here. We can only dislike people that we are really interested in. We dislike them because we are afraid of them – which means that they are inducing a sort of negative hero-worship. We are lowered in our own estimation when we come across them because exactly the same process of projection is occurring, this time in a negative way. It is an indication that something inside us is still badly wanting to grow. When we accept the fact, and have the courage to find out why, we unlock further resources in our make-up.

We become aware that we are at the receiving end of other people's projections, helping them, or not helping them, to grow in their turn. Can they disclose to us what they are thinking and feeling? Have we so grown in judgment and understanding that we can help them to get free? To be honest with oneself is the only passport which admits across the frontier of anyone else's life, to get past the outward screen which the face presents, to the real person behind the screen. It was to create this kind of relationship that Christ brought his friends together and brought his Church into being.

Through it all I am a self, because I am a self in relationship, and I discover what I am, in this sort of way. If I am still partly buried in other people, I can only live at a superficial level. I am then a colourless conformist, who takes his colour from his surroundings, and is unduly dependent on a favourable environment: we are all spiritual chameleons to some extent. But then some misfortune or failure, some rejection or betrayal, which we thought an irretrievable disaster at the time, throws us back on our resources and we find that we have more strength than we thought we had. We wonder afterwards how on earth we ever got through, but 'we learned through our sufferings'.

3. Two ways of knowing

Here then are two ways or types of knowing. I see the outside of things with my eyes and I am drawn to a deeper understanding of other human beings through my feelings. Do these two ways of knowing draw together at any point?

They begin to do so when we realise that they are complementary and never occur separately. What I think of as my mind, is a superstructure, erected on a deeper awareness of feeling. I learn through my eyes and take this process very much for granted, but the unhappy child cannot learn, and its mental development is stunted by its retarded emotional life. The baby that is not loved may even die and the child that is deprived of affection may become a psychopath. It is always true that 'the heart has its reasons which the mind knows not of!'

Feelings cannot grow unless they are brought into contact with other people, and we make sense of our feelings by bringing them out into the open and seeing what sort of people we are reacting to. When we do not see this clearly we become emotionally confused, experience physical symptoms that have no organic cause, and are caught in a state of conflict because we cannot sort things out. Knowledge is the upper level of experience, and feeling the deeper level. Some of us have well-trained intellects and less developed feelings; others of us allow our hearts to rule our heads. When the old rabbi said that 'a man's inwardness should equal his outwardness', he was trying to hold the balance between the head and the heart.

We need to be reminded of this. Our modern emphasis on the education of the mind can be misleading. The body of the modern child is well fed, and his mind may be well stocked with information, but we are apt to forget that there is a deeper element in him which needs feeding too. When the heart is empty of affection, the strong body and the ingenious mind may well produce a dangerous criminal rather than an honest citizen. The decline of personal religion makes this only too likely.

I do not believe that the position of religion today is worse than in the past. We are so apt to look at the past through rose-coloured spectacles and much that used to pass for religion was only conformity accepted by the chameleons of society because they could not think for themselves. Real religion has always been a rare commodity – as rare perhaps as real art or true science. Further progress depends not on some mass conversion of the indifferent, but on finding a new way of looking at things.

Here we are held up by the lack of any new ideas and we are almost afraid to think. We have been told so often that the universe is empty and we must not 'project' on to it, or read into it, anything remotely corresponding to our own feelings, in the supposed interest of 'scientific objectivity'.

The argument about projection rests upon a misunderstanding of what projection is. It is one thing to say that I project a wrong image on to another human being; this is happening all the time. If something goes wrong with the relationship I should have had with my father or mother, I carry that problem over into my relationships with other people. In this way a man can project a 'divided mother image' on to two people, the wife whom he idolises, and the woman he despises. This is understandable but no one projects his father or mother image on to nothing at all. This line of argument is not very sound.

Let us try again, and go back to the point we started from – the distinction between observation from outside and feeling from inside. When I look at you, I see only your outside (even when I look into your brain). You, on the other hand, are the only person who can feel your own feelings. The light that strikes the retina of your eyes triggers off an impulse which travels to your brain; you experience this as a blue sky or a green field. This is the outside and the inside of experience. Somehow these two basic facts fit together, but no one can say how. This is the central problem in all attempts to understand the why and how of things.

We just have to assume that the electrical happening in your brain (which I can see or detect), conforms with the picture which is forming in your mind (which you see, and I don't). We take this solution completely for granted every day of our lives, but it is still beyond any sort of explanation.

If the scientist tries to be objective, by concentrating exclusively on the outside picture and leaving out the inside, the picture inevitably loses meaning: this is just what is happening in our modern world, and is the main reason for the decline of religious faith.

4. Physical light and spiritual light

We can narrow the problem down a little further by following clues in a number of directions. The fact is obvious that we are entirely part of the universe which we are trying to understand. We have, it is true, grown a long way mentally and emotionally from our nearest neighbours in the animal world, but the prodigious development which has taken place in us is a growth out of what was there already, at a lower level of complexity. Continuity runs through the whole line of evolution. Much has been developed, but no new ingredient has been added.

This means that we are driven to assume that 'mind' in some primitive form, has been in existence in 'matter' all along. 'Self consciousness' is its latest development, and we are not reading this back into the lowliest specks of life. Even to these we must attribute some kind of awareness that makes 'behaviour' possible.

But can we stop there? We cannot very well do so, for chemically and physically there is no dividing line between what we (for convenience) call alive or not-alive. It is all made up of the same basic structure of molecules and atoms and nuclei. The only observable difference is that life is a more complex form of not-life.

The closer we investigate the structure of things the more complicated the puzzle becomes. Everything turns out on closer examination to be so very empty. Matter is very tightly packed. An ounce of lead, for instance, contains something like 23,000 million million million atoms, if that figure means anything to you, but there is so little actual matter within this apparent denseness. The molecules in my brain are made up of atoms, are made up of subatomic particles, are made up of 'resonances'; to quote Jeans' famous simile, the amount of solid matter in the atom corresponds to half -a-dozen wasps circling in an otherwise empty Waterloo station. Ultimately I seem to be an elaborate sort of sponge, or perhaps a honey-comb, or should I borrow the schoolboy's definition of a net, as 'a number of holes tied together'?

What am I then? The mystery deepens when I realise that no particle of matter in me is in touch with any other particle. This 'too solid flesh' is not even in contact with the chair I am sitting on; if it was, I should become part of the chair, not even the bits and pieces of my brain are in contact. What connects them is a form of energy and this energy is best described as a form of light. It is part of the wide waveband of light which I am unable to see. Matter itself has been described as 'congealed light'. Whatever else I may be, I am the result of light, in one way or another.

This is much what religious people have been saying for a long, long time. Whenever we want to talk about mind or describe mental processes, we are always forced back to some word which is descriptive of light. The realisation of truth is naturally thought of as a moment of illumination. When our ideas come into focus, we feel that light has dawned. Christ used it as an analogy of spiritual illumination and integration: 'when thine eye is single, thy whole body is full of light'. Is this a clue to the meaning of things? Is this what we really mean when we detect a nervous impulse travelling from the retina to the brain? Is it part of the phenomenon of light? Is this where the ways meet?

5. Time, energy and resonance

There are other puzzles in plenty. What about time? Why is it that we *see* space in three dimensions, but *feel* the passage of time (the fourth dimension, which cannot be separated from the other three)? Is time the mental factor in our experience? We cannot know or feel except in time, as we only experience process and change. Here is another curious fact to consider, that in some way light annihilates time. As light travels at an infinite (or limiting) velocity, it arrives as soon as it sets out, for it loses no time on the way, nor does it lose any energy. A photon of light crosses the universe and (provided that it does not intercept anything on the way) arrives with the same energy that it starts off with. As a famous physicist put it, it is rather like throwing a plank off a ship in the Indian Ocean, watching it travel under its own impetus half way round the world till it hits a ship in the Atlantic, jumps out of the ocean and comes to a standstill on the deck.

Does this give a new twist to the idea of 'eternal', or a new glimpse of what words like mind and time might mean? As we are in time, we lose time and experience it – for us light that has left the sun and is striking our eyes, has taken eight minutes to get here. This is just as true as the previous statement, for this is a relative universe in which every point of view is equally valid.

Another peculiarity of the universe is its fantastic sensitivity. One heavenly body 'feels' another across the yawning gulf of empty space and no one can offer any reasonable explanation of this. We can understand 'forces': if I strike a billiard ball, it hits another, and so on. The Middle Ages called this 'a force from behind'. Attraction is a 'force from in front' and this makes no sense. Whitehead had no hesitation in ascribing 'feeling' as awareness to matter, as Francis Bacon had done before him. Many people would be shocked by this, but only habit and prejudice stand in the way of our accepting the idea.

There is another curious fact that is worth mentioning – the energy of empty space. Apparently the energy locked up in matter – in our own earth, for example – would drain out into space, but space is already charged with energy and cannot take any more. The very diffuse energy which is distributed through 'empty' space, offsets the energy locked up in matter and so the earth survives. Evidently 'matter' is crammed into a very small space, and needs a good deal of compensating emptiness to keep it where it is.

In one way or another it is difficult to resist the conclusion that the physicist has come to the end of matter and is beginning to come to grips with mind. If one was looking for a definition of mind, could one do better than describe it as weightless, immaterial energy? Is it true that 'the things that are seen' are contributed to, or formed by, 'the things that are not seen'? We come back again to a basically religious point of view.

If science explores the outside of things, it is the task of religion to explore the inside. One is reminded again of the many attempts that have been made in the past to make sense of this emptiness. Perhaps 'being' can best be described in negative terms; the idea of 'nothing' has traditionally been a fruitful way of opening up a constructive line of thought about reality. The form which it is taking now, is to realise that 'objects' are of less significance than the fields of force that surround them and give rise to them. Space may be more important than matter.

At this point the idea of resonance is a help. If I strike a piano key, a china ornament starts to ring. This is a familiar experience; but the whole structure of things is based on the same basic phenomenon. We are familiar with it in another everyday happening. The oscillations in the transmitting aerial at the broadcasting station cause a similar disturbance in my receiving aerial (as it also does in the wiring of my electric bell, in the iron frame of my bedstead, or in the tree outside my window). I can tune in to the station, and I can amplify the signals by the simple device of broadcasting on the same wavelength. Sooner or later we shall be driven to recognise that there is a comparable 'induction of emotion' between human beings, especially in a group or a crowd – one need only think of the panic which sweeps through a theatre at the cry of 'fire'! We can understand what someone else is feeling if it rouses an answering chord in ourselves. Sometimes we are trying hard to understand, but although we search our experience we cannot find anything which seems to correspond to this. This is likely to be true of the nervous, the anti-social or the sufferer from intense pain. The answer comes from inside ourselves or not at all: when we understand we realize that we are sympathizing 'on the same wavelength', as it were.

Are there deeper resonances than this which we think of in terms of prayer and spiritual experience? Human beings have always believed so: have believed that their more complex endowment of mind has enabled them to sort out the deeper under-currents of feeling that lie beneath (but are an integral part of) everyday experience. It is so often assumed that religion reaches up into the sky and is always an outgoing process. In fact the opposite is true. One has only to think of St Theresa urging her nuns to find the inmost room in their spiritual castle; or St John of the Cross pointing the way that lies to the deepest centre in our lives as the well of divine love; or St Augustine telling us in the Confessions that the Holy Spirit was guiding him to look inside himself; or St Anselm or St Bernard analysing the nature of real love as the path to Christ, to see how misguided many of our ideas about religion can be. It is this discovery of what lies within us that leads the way to a better understanding of what lies outside us, and discovering what it all means. What we are discovering is the real meaning of 'love' and the more we reflect upon it, the less possible is it to think of 'love' as confined to ourselves.

Religion is primarily the disclosure of what is already there, within myself – called in traditional language (which I do not propose to alter) the presence of God (in Christian thinking, the Holy Spirit); but we need not worry unduly about a form of words. It opens up for the religious man an awareness of meaning, the conviction that the inside picture of things is being unrolled.

6. Some religious ideas

Two other ideas may briefly be mentioned. Many people are worried by the apparent contradiction between the scientific picture of the universe in which every event is 'determined' and the religious belief in freedom. Again I think that these ideas come together very convincingly in Christ's teaching. One need only think of a passage like Matt 5:45, where the love of God is compared to the sunshine that is given to all men equally. The point here is that love is true to itself, and is as invariable as any scientific law. (It has been claimed that this Christian view of the consistency of God really made an ordered science possible.)

I used to think that the planets moved round the sun like trams on fixed tramlines, at a regular speed. Now I realise that they are infinitely sensitive to the pull and tug of every other planet within range; this is the scientific equivalent of the religious man's idea of the love that moves the sun and all the stars! Somewhere there must be a correspondence between these two ways of looking at things (and this must come from the religious side).

Another religious difficulty that keeps cropping up concerns the relationship of God to the individual. Does an omnipotent God control all men's endeavours? This is a hangover from an earlier age, as between Calvinist predestination and scientific determinism there is no moral difference. Many readers of St John's Gospel, for instance, think of the person of Christ as a sort of puppet controlled from on high. Needless to say, this is not the impression which St John is trying to give. He sees Christ as a man so bursting with the divine love and compassion – dare we call it an ability to resonate? – that it flows out of him at any excuse and on every occasion. He found within himself the resources to be 'in tune' with human beings of every kind.

This is the idea behind the phrase 'Son of Man', which is used by Christ to indicate that he thinks of his whole people as belonging to him and being part of his 'body'. (In Hebrew thinking the body is not only the physical self but the wider, emotional self, or the self in relationship to the family, the social group, or to Jews everywhere.) This is a natural extension of the ordinary idea of personality as we understand it, but then our ideas are rather narrow. It is entirely in line with the picture of the personality emerging gradually through 'projection'. We find in belonging to others what we ourselves really are.

7. Some concluding reflections

Sir Winston Churchill once remarked that to see clearly into the future one first had to look back into the past. A sense of historical perspective can certainly be a great help. The problem of science and religion has been swinging to and fro for a long time.

In 1100 St Anselm was delving into his inner mind to work out the meaning of the word 'being', and in 1200 St Bernard was working out the implications of 'love' (in a very modern manner). They were the leaders in a movement of personal devotion which has been the strength and weakness of Western Christianity ever since. The tradition of accurate analysis laid down in those years became the foundation on which science was later to be built. Then theology took a wrong turning, and gave up the central premise of Christian thinking – the presence of the Holy Spirit within the human heart. (The early Church could never have sung a hymn like 'Come, Holy Ghost . . .' It would have been considered blasphemous.) The revised theology, put forward in a masterly manner by Aquinas, was fought bitterly by his opponents (Bonaventure and others) who saw that it was bound to lead to the growing scepticism of the next two centuries: God was wholly 'other' and therefore unknowable. The older tradition was kept alive in the remarkable flowering of personal religion in the Rhineland and the Netherlands, to pass later into the tradition of the Jesuits and the Spanish Carmelites, St Theresa and St John of the Cross. The Reformation in N Europe was a revolt against this scepticism, and an attempt to return to the classic theology of the 'Indwelling Spirit'.

Scepticism reached another peak in England in the thoroughgoing materialism of Hobbes (1651), who reduced all thinking to the movement of 'some internal substance in the head', but his remarkable anticipation of modern thinking was offset by the Cambridge Platonists and the Society of Friends (the return of 'the inner light'). Although this spiritual insight was confirmed by such influential writers and propagandists as William Law and John Wesley, its intellectual content was not enough to swing the pendulum back the other way. God was still pushed out of his universe by a long line of thinkers, like Newton (who fancied himself as a theologian) and the Deists; and the 'outside view' and the 'inside view' were still kept far apart. Materialism reached its zenith about 1875, by which time it looked as if religion had taken a knockout blow. The publication of Darwin's Origin of Species established the idea of evolution and upset the compromise which most thinkers had accepted since Newton, of the clockmaker who had wound up the universe in the beginning and was letting it run down.

Once again there was a return to the classic principles of theology. Scientific materialism was subjected to rigorous logical scrutiny by Martineau and others, and its inner inconsistencies exposed. This led to a rising tide of 'idealism', a movement which went far to re-establish basic religious ideas, but burnt itself out after the First World War. Hegel had been its prophet and his ideas had borne some unhappy children, including Marxism, and the deification of the State (and also, incidentally, Christian Science). This was another wrong turning, from which our thinking has not fully recovered. In the meantime there has been a scientific revolution: the materialism which seemed to have carried the day in 1875, now looks very different, thanks to

Einstein and a host of subsequent discoveries. A revival of theology is overdue. I have no doubt it is on its way, but perhaps the way is not yet fully prepared for it.

CHAPTER SIXTEEN

God,
a New Look

'Ask, or you won't get anything. Search, or you won't find. Hammer on the door, or nobody will open it for you.' Christ said that faith is a quest, which reminded him of a man who was certain that treasure was buried in a field and dug it all up until he found it. Faith is childlike (not childish) and the hallmark of a healthy child is endless curiosity. It has been said of the good scientist that he has never given up his childhood curiosity. That should be even more true of religion. If religion gives up asking questions, it ceases to be true religion and becomes only a fossilised faith. The cynical French writer Anatole France once wrote: 'God has preserved his saints from thinking'. I hope that is not true of you.

Religion in our own day is waking up and entering a new phase of exploration and discovery. Till 1500 the Church laid down the law about faith and no one questioned it. Then the Bible became the touchstone of faith and no one questioned that. But science had been growing and doubt had been creeping in. When Darwin and others proved that the world was not created in seven days, much of the Bible was seen to be poetic rather than historical. Now we are in a scientific age and for a long time it looked as if science and religion were on a collision course and that science was winning. That is not true today, as many of the old difficulties have been removed. One example will suffice.

When I was a young man (after the First War) it was taken for granted in scientific circles that 'mind' was an illusion. We were completely controlled by the iron laws of nature which left no room for 'me'. 'Purpose' was a dirty word in biology. As an eminent philosopher-mathematician remarked at the time, it was curious to see so many purposive scientists trying so hard to prove that purpose did not exist. Now all that has changed. Life is now seen to be made up of countless acts of choice. 'Life is selection', they say nowadays – a great advance on what was said before. A famous neurologist has remarked that nature's greatest gift to man is the ability to pause; ie not to react instinctively or immediately but to pause and select our response. For instance, we do not always have to be angry with someone who is angry with us; we can remember the old copybook saying 'a soft answer turneth away wrath'. That is one of the reasons why we learn to relax; it restores our 'initiative' so that we are not at the mercy of the situation but 'on top of it' once more.

Can we imagine what God is like? No, and yes. For the same reason that we cannot imagine what the atom is like; science is helping us here too. The famous physicist Richard Feynman used to give introductory lectures on physics (which are used by students everywhere). Half way through the course he would stop and ask them if they could imagine what they were thinking about, and showed them it was quite impossible. An electron may have a spin or half a spin (what on earth is that?) and the theorist is reduced to using words like colour and strangeness to describe aspects of the electron for which he has a mathematical formula. Sub-atomic particles are real enough but totally unimaginable. It is the same with God. We have reasons for talking about God as we do, but after a time words fail us. We use a word like 'personal' because God cannot have qualities that are less than personal, but this does not mean that God is a sort of Father Christmas sitting on a cloud somewhere.

That is why Christ told his friends: 'no one has seen God at any time' but he also told them –'if you have seen me, you have seen the Father'. The point is that we do not see God but feel him. Christ felt him so deeply that he called God 'Abba' which is the affectionate, family word for father. The first Christians were taught to use the word to make sure that they thought of God as very close to them, not a remote far away God who is not interested in humans. It is words like infinite and almighty that get in the way here. People used to think of God as up in the sky. Then they thought of him outside the solar system, or in the remote depths of space. All that has become ridiculous.

We have to balance that idea of God by moving in the opposite direction. When I think of 'infinity' I think of God not only as infinitely great but as infinitely small – the kind of poetic fantasy that the poet William Blake indulged in when he wrote 'To see a World in a grain of sand, and a Heaven in a wild flower, Hold Infinity in the palm of your hand, and Eternity in an hour.' (Songs of Innocence). You see – you can reach infinity by adding 1 + 2 + 3 ... or you can go the other way: 1, $^1/_2$, $^1/_4$ and so on. In other words, space-words do not apply to God.

This is what the scientists have been doing. Instead of looking into reality with a telescope, they have used a microscope and looked at the infinitely small, which seems to be a new world with its own rules. What fascinates me is the amount of power that is locked up in this other end of infinity. When you fall down the stairs and land heavily at the bottom, you complain bitterly about the force of gravity, but gravity is the weakest force known to the scientist. The forces which bind the nucleus of the atom together are millions of times stronger than gravity. These are the forces which hold your brain together; without 'infinity' at this end of the scale, we should not exist at all! So do remember that we are not looking at all this from outside, like looking at strange fish in an aquarium. We are in this completely. These forces hold your brain and mine together, and in them we 'live and move and have our being'. Everything we are and everything we have has emerged from in here. It is not surprising therefore that the spiritually wise, not only in Christianity, have looked inside themselves to find God – not 'out there but in here'.

There is more in this than just an idea. Look at it in this way. The startling discoveries of the last hundred years show us that the conscious mind is only the tip of an iceberg; every moment of the day and night our conscious minds are fed from below somewhere by a constant flow of thoughts, feelings, wishes, impulses, the highs and lows of elation and depression, of love and hate, and we are entirely dependent on this inner flow. It does not happen just automatically, we choose these thoughts, (at least in their general direction), 'suppressing' some and encouraging others, so that the thrust is kept in focus by our general view of life. As I tell people when they are relaxing, 'you can come into life with an open hand or with a clenched fist'. Many of us are squeezed up into ourselves by all the hurts and disappointments we have suffered at different times. We are motivated more often than we realise by our desire to get our own back on somebody. Spiritual freedom – the freedom to enjoy our own lives – depends on believing that love is more important than hate, which is why Christ called for forgiveness all round. The question which faces all of us is simply what attitude do I take up towards the world and its problems. I hate suffering and pain and I can avoid suffering in one of two ways. I can be a stoic or a good timer. We can train ourselves not to feel, in the hope of being impervious to 'all the slings and arrows of outrageous fortune' and steel ourselves against suffering. A lot of people in the caring professions do this; they see so much that is upsetting that they could hardly carry on at all if they 'weakened'. People at the other end of the scale make up their minds to forget the sad side of life as much as they can and plunge into any sort of enjoyment that is available to them. They are the 'non-carers' (so long as it gives them an escape from life). As T S Eliot remarked: 'man cannot bear too much reality'.

Love is the food of this inner 'me' which traditionally we call the 'heart', because we recognise that our feelings lie deeper than our words. As the French writer Pascal put it three hundred years ago, 'the heart has reasons which the mind knows not of'. Religion is concerned with the heart, because religion believes that love is at the heart of everything. Modern research knows this only too well; children need love ('attachments') or they do not flourish (our prisons are full of people who have never known what real love is like).

Love is the food of 'me'. Christ called it 'bread from heaven' – 'I have food to eat that you know not of'. God feeds us with deeper ideas of love if we can respond to love and grow more loving – that is to say, more like the love of God. Or we can put it very simply in this way. We all need food for the body and more light than we have ever seen before. Our courage creeps back and our curiosity again comes into its own. The trouble is that as a result of two world wars and other difficulties, we have lost something of our faith, and in face of the many dangers that threaten civilisation, we have lost our nerve. We need a new look at 'God' – a new look at love and what love really demands. For many people serious illness can be an experience of this kind; people have survived concentration camps by clinging to this inner faith.

It cannot be said too often that 'salvation' is not deliverance *from* every evil or disaster which may befall us but *through* it; through suffering to insight, through darkness to light, through the Cross to the Resurrection. We join the vast army of suffering humanity working for what Christ called 'the Kingdom of God' (the rule of love in the world). At heart you are part of that army, or you would not find your way into His church.

Our picture of the world has altered all too dramatically in my lifetime. When I was a small boy, I had a lovely atlas (one of my most cherished possessions) which had a map of the solar system with the planets going round the sun. I imagined that they kept to rigid paths, like trams on tramlines. They do, but they are infinitely sensitive. I realised this when I read that the same astronomer, Jeans, took his small niece out into the garden at night and made her shake her fist at the moon to convince her that whatever she did, had an effect on a distant object like the moon. I thought he was mad, but now this is a commonplace. Endless TV programmes on the science of chaos ('chaology') tell us that small incidents can have enormous consequences. New ideas about gravity attract me; tiny particles draw closer to each other across the vast emptiness of space and so draw the moon nearer the earth, and so on. That is what I believe about prayer. When I am praying for someone who is ill, I am sure that I draw closer to them, and support them, and give them strength and courage and – sometimes at least – physical strength as well. This gives me tremendous encouragement (and them too).

In the new physics, forces depend on fields; ie any object (like the earth) is surrounded by 'empty space', by the field of energy which supports it. What we see grows out of what we do not see. A New Testament writer said this first: 'What is seen was made out of things not seen'(Hebrews 11:3). In religion we believe that we are sensitive to what is unseen.

I used to think of the universe as a cold, insensitive place. Matter is infinitely sensitive to other matter; this is a universe of 'attraction'. If one set out to imagine a universe which expressed the nature of a sensitive deity, this universe would be the result. 'The heavens declare the glory of God' wrote the Psalmist; they probably do, much more than we realise. The same poet went on to write that he felt this same sensitivity (which he thought of as the law of God) working in him, and prayed that it might do so more effectively. Christ felt that the love of God was the answer to the needs of man. A great writer, St Augustine, wrote that we are sponges in the ocean of divine love and the water flows through the sponge. He summed it up in words that make a wonderful prayer:

'Eternal God, the light of the minds that know thee, the joy of the hearts that love thee, the strength of the wills that serve thee: grant us so to know thee that we may truly love thee, so to love that we may fully serve thee, whose service is perfect freedom, through Jesus Christ our Lord.'

CHAPTER SEVENTEEN

The Revival
of the
Healing Ministry

Historical

Christ founded His Church to carry on His work, and that work was clearly defined by one of its earliest writers as 'preach the gospel and heal the sick'. It is naturally to be expected that an altered spiritual outlook will lead to a changed physical condition. Christ demonstrated this at the outset of His ministry when a paralysed man was brought to Him by four friends who let their friend down through a hole in the roof of the house where Christ was staying. Christ first told the sick man that God had forgiven him and then told him to carry his bed home. It was said of Christ that He went about doing good and healing every kind of disease among the people, and the gospel record contains a long series of such healings.

For four hundred years or more after His death the Church carried on His work in the same way. Prayers for the sick were prayers for healing, not prayers for the passive acceptance of disease. Such a prayer (taken from the Sacramentary of Serapion, c 350 AD) contains language of this kind: 'send forth healing power (from Christ) . . . for the chasing away of every fever and shivering fit and every infirmity, for good grace and remission of sins, for a medicine of life and salvation, for health and complete wholeness of mind, body, spirit, for complete strengthening . . .'

This is the language of complete conviction. There is no doubt here that health of the whole personality is the gift of God, and that it is God's will to bestow it. It is remarkable that the entire literature of the early Church seems to reflect the same attitude. Irenaeus, Bishop of Lyons (who lost his life in the persecution of 202 AD) could assert in his day that 'those who have been cleansed from all evil spirits frequently both believe in Christ and join the Church; others heal the sick by laying their hands upon them and they are made whole . . . It is not possible to enumerate the gifts which the Church, spread abroad throughout the whole world, has received from God in the name of Jesus Christ and which she uses every single day for the benefit of the non-Christian, deceiving no one and taking no reward from them' (Quoted by Miss Evelyn Frost, Christian Healing, p 65.)

Tertullian writing at Rome about 200 AD claimed that healing through the Christian Church was well known to the authorities of his day, and even declared that the emperor Severus had been anointed and had received healing.

As long as the undivided Church remained true to the prayer of Christ, that they may be one, even as we are one, it retained the fullness of its spiritual power, but by the middle of the third century a warning note was being struck by St Cyprian of Carthage (who lost his life in the persecution of 257 AD): 'No longer was there that united solidarity in face of a pagan world, but differences of opinion, division and moral laxity had crept in, thereby weakening the power of the Church'.

Cyprian, acutely alive to this, says that had not the Church fallen into division and sin, persecution would not have arisen, or if it had arisen, it would at once have been ended through the power of the witness of the Church and her prevailing power in prayer, prevailing because united . . . 'While we despised the commandments of the Lord . . . the enemy was receiving a power of doing mischief, and was overwhelming . . . those who were imperfectly armed and too careless to resist.'

The prevailing power in prayer which was lacking to overcome persecution was likewise lacking to heal the sick and raise the dead (Frost, pp 68-9). St Augustine, writing a 150 years later, after Christianity had become the official religion of the empire, could speak from personal experience of miracles of healing, but regretted the fact that so many people could read the stories in the gospels without applying them to their own needs.

In his day the flood tide of barbarian invasion had already begun to overwhelm Western Europe, and the Church began to lose its desire to heal. Gregory the Great, writing about 600 AD welcomed the plague that was devastating Italy as it would save so many from a worse fate at the hands of their enemies (C Dawson, *Making of Europe*, p 150). It is not surprising that the Church lost its first triumphant attitude to physical sickness, or that a little later Columbanus, the founder of a monastery in the Vosges, should approve of self torture as a regular spiritual exercise. The body was no longer honoured as 'the temple of the Spirit' but despised as the source of weakness and corruption. Even so, the Church continued to expect the healing of sickness to occur, but only as an exceptional event, as a relaxation of God's real will as it were, which is to be contrasted with the attitude of the early Church. It became the rule of the Church in the Middle Ages to recognise as saints only those who were known to have been the means of healing of at least two sick people in their lifetime, and the number of such canonisations is evidence of the belief and practice of the Church. It must not be forgotten too that the Eastern Church has retained its tradition of healing.

So much for the belief and attitude of the Church; the question then arises, what means did the Church employ? It cannot be too strongly stressed at the outset that this, like everything else which the Church did, was regarded as the work of the whole Church. It is the whole Church, in every place that the Church meets, which is the Body of Christ, coming together Sunday by Sunday (the weekly anniversary of the Resurrection) to renew its fellowship with Christ, to realise His Presence and His power, to pray together and manifest that power as light in a dark world. 'Member' means literally 'limb', and the members of the Church were limbs of Christ's Body; if they were absent from the weekly gathering, the Body of Christ was maimed and incomplete and its spiritual power defective. Division and disharmony among its members, with the breaking of the commandment to 'love one another', was thwarting the work of the Spirit. Healing is a work of 'making whole', and a Church that is not whole can only partly manifest this power of wholeness; that problem must always be before our minds.

The life-giving, healing power of the Spirit is manifested or diffused through the members of the Body. The Source of Life – to the early Church – was this making real the Body of Christ, through which the members received 'the Bread of Heaven in Christ Jesus', and believed that they were, in Ignatius' words, the 'medicine of immortality'. This was their service, to renew the New Covenant, as Christ had commanded them to do. To remain 'in Spirit' they took with them from that service in a little silver box a fragment of the consecrated bread; partaking of this every morning they could be one in Spirit with all other members of the Body. At this service the sick were blessed in the presence of the whole Church, the mentally afflicted 'exorcised', and the prayer of the whole Church was offered on their behalf. If possible, the sick were brought to the Church, on beds and litters, and it is stated in one document that the 'healing of the sick depends on their coming frequently to church, and enjoying (corporate) prayer.' Where this was not possible, bishop, clergy and laity, with the choir, were directed to hold a service twice a day at the bedside of the sick person. It will be seen again how constantly the emphasis was placed on the prayer of the whole Church, rather than upon the faith of the individual sufferer, though he was also expected to play his part.

At the bedside the sick person was ministered to by anointing with oil, with the laying on of hands, with exorcism and prayer for the breaking of all evil influences. Christ had sent His disciples in pairs to go from village to village to anoint the sick and 'cast out demons'. St James (5:14) lays upon the individual the duty to call in the Church to his help: 'Is any among you sick? Let him call for the elders of the Church, and let them pray over him, anointing him with oil in the name of the Lord; and the prayer of faith will save the sick man, and the Lord will raise him up, and if he has committed sin, he will be forgiven.' In practice the anointing with oil (unction) and the laying on of hands were given together, during which the sick person was encouraged to get up and kneel by his bed: 'Here let all the priests and their assistants lay their hands upon the sick man'. Then followed unction: 'Let him (ie the Bishop or priest appointed by the Bishop) thoroughly anoint the sick man with consecrated oil, on the neck and throat, and between the shoulders and upon the breast; and let him be more thoroughly and liberally anointed where the pain is more threatening. And let the sick man pray while he is being anointed, and let one of the priests recite this prayer: "I anoint thee with holy oil in the name of the Father, and of the Son, and of the Holy Ghost, that no unclean spirit may be hid in thee, or in thy limbs, or in the marrow (of thy bones) or in any joint of thy limbs, but that the power of Christ most high and of the Holy Ghost may dwell in thee . . ." '

A further prayer besought God to 'expel all forms of vain glory, to heal the ancient scars of conscience, to expel inordinate passions, to restore the substance of flesh and blood, and to grant pardon of all sins.' The sick man would then make his communion. It was also the custom to bless the sick man's medicine, his food, and the water he drank. Oil blessed by the Church could be used by the sufferer and his family to anoint him at home.

One of the delights of reading the kind of prayer which the early Church would use in such a situation is to realise again how very comprehensive was their understanding of the problem. One feels that the modern literature on the emotional background of disease would have been no surprise to them. Their whole attitude seems to show a sturdy commonsense.

One imagines that this robust attack on the problem of disease would have been of the greatest spiritual value to the patient and one can hardly over-emphasise the spiritual comfort and support the patient would receive from knowing that the whole Church was behind him.

The medical approach

Since Pasteur discovered germs, the main attention of medicine has been directed towards the causes of disease which attack the body from outside. By eliminating some, or finding antidotes for others, fantastic progress has been made. It would be impossible for most of us even to imagine the state of things which existed in this country only a century ago. Most of the great scourges which have terrified mankind in the past have been stamped out in all parts of the world where medicine is free to counter them effectively. For this magnificent achievement we should be devoutly thankful.

To the onlooker it now seems that medicine is moving into a new phase; or some would say that it is returning to an old one. The very success of medicine has created a new situation. It has eliminated the plagues, but left the kind of disease which creeps on the sufferer insidiously and is apt to leave him in a condition of chronic ill-health. As such diseases are not obviously caused by a germ or a virus, they cannot be countered by the methods which have succeeded so well in the past. Heart disease, rheumatism, gastric ulcer, diseases of nervous origin, for example, seem to fall into this group, and there are many others in which, even if there is a physical cause present, non-physical causes play a prominent part. Medicine in America first coined the word 'psychosomatic' to express this new concept of disease.

If I suffer from anxiety for many years, for instance, it is only too likely that I shall experience in permanent form the physical changes which anxiety tends to produce. When I feel frightened, the muscles below the diaphragm contract in order to drive the blood from my digestive organs into my limbs, and digestion is abruptly halted. Nature makes me ready almost instantaneously for violent action. My heart beats faster, my lungs breathe more quickly, in order to sustain this effort. The muscles involved in movement are equally tense, and sugar is released in the muscles to provide me with additional energy. Many minor changes also occur; my skin contracts, to render loss of blood less likely in the event of a wound, and blood clots more easily, for the same reason. If my hair no longer stands on end, like a cat's fur when its anger is aroused, it is still true that I tend to frown horribly – originally a device of nature to strike fear into my enemies and make actual fighting unnecessary – and this does my eyes no good. More important, I can no longer concentrate voluntarily on whatever I was thinking about before I was frightened. Nature insists that I should think only of attack and defence, or flight. For the same reason I am exceptionally wide awake, and keep looking round.

Fear, as fear, is a beautiful device of Nature to deliver us from emergencies of every kind. In the ordinary way we should act at once, as we leap out of the way of an advancing motorcar, and the emotional and physical changes are rapidly worked off. But in the modern world mild fear in the form of anxiety and stress is with us all the time, and therefore these reactions are constantly occurring. Our digestion is always being interfered with; it is hardly surprising if it becomes permanently disturbed. Our hearts are always beating too fast, and as the heart has to adjust itself to this strain, a chronic condition is set up. Our muscles are in a chronic state of tension, which means that the circulation is affected; the tiny, hair-like capillaries through which the blood has to pass from the arteries to the veins are more or less permanently squeezed, with the result – natural enough when you think it out – that in many parts of the body the cells are not receiving the oxygen which is necessary to their life, or the food which they need to support life, and the blood cannot take away the waste products of the process. Fatigue means that our muscles are clogged with these waste products, which the circulation cannot clear. All this sets up a condition of dis-ease, in which the body is much more open to attack from outside. Similar reactions in the skin, and the internal surfaces of the body which resemble the skin, are responsible for a further group of diseases which medicine still finds extremely difficult to treat, characterised by extreme irritation and sensitivity.

The effects on the mind are also far-reaching. One of the most distressing effects of what we call loosely 'nerves' is the loss of concentration, which (as we have seen) is the normal effect of fear. Another effect is insomnia; when we are frightened, we are on the 'qui vive', however tired we are, and sleep is out of the question. These very common symptoms of fear cause more trouble than many physical ailments, especially when they are not understood and are taken by the sufferer to be the early symptoms of mental breakdown. It is not surprising that the national drug bill is considerable.

The modern doctor is thus paying more and more attention to the effect of the emotions on our physical condition. The negative emotions of anxiety and fear undermine health; the opposite qualities of confidence and curiosity, which are the qualities of a healthy child, strengthen the will to live. So much is fairly obvious. What is not at all obvious, and left to ourselves we should probably never suspect it, is that the worst damage in our bodies is done by the emotions which we do *not* feel. Our chronic habit of putting all unpleasant thoughts out of our minds drives the emotion down into our bodies where it becomes a most effective agent in causing disease. The irritation, which it would be wrong for us to feel, appears as an irritation of the skin or of some part of the body, like the lungs, which grew from the skin. Anything to do with affection can influence the heart and its action most strongly, though the connection may not be easy to trace. The contempt and scorn of others, especially when we are young and spiritually defenceless, undermines our natural confidence and can cause emotional and physical suffering all through life.

Sometimes the physical symptom is a clue to its spiritual cause. Life can so easily become a headache when we cannot solve its problems; and the experiences which we cannot swallow are rejected by the stomach as well as by the mind. Probably there are few diseases in ordinary experience which do not reflect a life situation of long standing. This may even be true of cancer, at least in some of its forms. A famous surgeon has claimed that we are all potentially cancerous in later life, but none of us incur the disease if we can preserve our freedom from stress. Here prevention is easier than cure. We need a hygiene of mind and spirit as well as body. We should clear our minds of apprehension and distrust, not by burying the unwanted emotion in the nervous system where it can do great harm to the life of the tissues which this nervous system organises and sustains, but by facing and accepting it with calm and courage. We should never underestimate 'the hygiene of a quiet mind'.

The spiritual approach

We cannot divide the human personality up into mind and body (regarded as two separate entities) as we once did. The materialism of our forebears is a dying creed, and the physical sciences are giving it its death-blow. The ten thousand million cells of the human brain comprise a vast mass of atoms made up of positive nucleus and negative electrons. To quote Jeans' famous simile, if the atoms were enlarged to the size of Waterloo station, the amount of solid matter within it would correspond to half a dozen wasps flying round inside; the rest is empty space. Yet this space, though empty of matter, is not empty in another sense. It has shape, for instance, and its shape determines what we used to call the force of gravity. It also possesses energy, for the energy of the material world is balanced by the energy of this immaterial world: they must be in a state of balance for matter to continue to exist, and there is a continuous exchange of energy between these two states which are thus interdependent. This balance of energy might be described as the basic law of the universe.

This space (or whatever we like to call it) carries the power of thought. Experiments in telepathy conducted by Rhine and others over the last 20 years have proved (to the satisfaction of all but a few die-hards) that communication can exist between minds over great distances. This cannot depend on any physical effect known to man, as it continues to take place when one of the experimenters is shielded by a wall of lead which would block the progress of any physical particle or wave. What then is this vast emptiness which is both inside and outside the physical world?

The religious man has no hesitation in answering the question. He has always been conscious, all down the ages, that there are two ways of knowledge. External knowledge comes to us through the senses, the eye in particular, which is now reinforced by every modern scientific device. I look at your body and see only its outside; with the help of x-rays I can see right through it, but I am still looking at it from outside, and this knowledge gives description but no meaning. I can detect, for example, an infinitesimal electric impulse (or something like it) travelling along a nerve, but I have no means of knowing that this is experienced by you as (let us say) a sharp pain, because knowledge gained through the senses cannot give me that information. But there is another avenue of knowledge, which we call feeling. If I am with someone who is violently frightened, I can feel and experience this fear. I cannot know what pain is, until I experience it myself; then I am sensitive to pain in others, and can interpret through my feelings what I perceive through my senses. The deeper my capacity for feeling, the more meaning I can discover in my experience.

There is thus, as we say metaphorically, a heart below the head, and as Pascal remarked, 'the heart has reasons of which reason is not aware'. We know more of the heart than Pascal did, and realise that if life is meaningless, it is because the 'mind' has cut itself off from the 'heart'. To the old way of prayer and meditation is being added the new way of psychology, through which religion is once more coming into its own.

But the way into what St Theresa called the 'Interior Castle' is blocked by weakness, fear and ignorance, wrong thinking and wrong doing of every kind. When we read the New Testament, we realise that Christ promised His friends the solution of these problems; the way of healing is the rediscovery of the answers which He gave. It is the way of feeling: 'love your neighbour as (part of) yourself; resist not evil; love your enemies, and so become sons of your Father in heaven'. Not to feel is to be 'without hope and without God' in the world – living, but only partly living. To feel is to suffer and, as the French proverb has it, to suffer is to die a little. Many are frightened of suffering probably because they confuse suffering with disease; the two are not the same; Christ suffered, but was not ill, and removed illness wherever He came across it. If we refuse suffering and spiritual pain, and believe that we shall be harmed by being hurt, we are refusing life itself. If we shut ourselves off from our fellow men, we can neither suffer nor sympathise with suffering, and we inevitably shut ourselves from the depths of our own hearts, and that means from God as well; there is then nothing left to do but to pursue sensation and call it pleasure.

To do this is to live life to ourselves. As time goes on it becomes less satisfying, more haunted by the ghosts of what might have been. We have many methods of escaping from reality. We shield ourselves with every protection that material circumstances can offer, with the kind of friends who will insulate us from real living or with beliefs which guard our self-confidence from the pricks of truth and conscience; beneath it all we have the heart, it may well be, of a frightened child. Does it help us to get what we want – money, position, security, or even the welfare state – if we are losing our soul? Life is gradually being lost, as Christ said it would be: 'he that saveth his life shall lose it'.

But to 'say no to oneself', to this little, petty, terrified self that is ruling our actions, but which is only a poor caricature of what God intended human nature to be – to do that is to take the heroic plunge (or baptism) into the way of suffering and sacrifice, of feeling and loving, of real living; to lose one's life and thus discover what life can mean. Suppose that instead of protecting ourselves against life and running away from experience we accept it, giving up our resistance to it, and abandoning our defences: what then? To our surprise life becomes much easier; as Christ said, 'My yoke is easy, and My burden is light'. It is easier because we no longer have to fight hard; easier because the road on which we are travelling will no longer wind so endlessly uphill. Our nerves will no longer be so perpetually at breaking point, and we are less likely to find open or hidden enemies on every hand. We can cope with difficulties as they arise and can permit the evil of today to be sufficient for today, not anticipating tomorrow's difficulties before they come, not dragging yesterday's difficulties into today, and not pushing today's into the distant future. It means too that we can live *with* people and share life with them, instead of living *for* them or *against* them; but that needs a word of explanation.

We tend in actual life to become fixed in one of two attitudes which might be described as the 'false child' and the 'false parent' Either we are doing everything for other people and nothing for ourselves, or everything for ourselves and nothing for others. In the first case we can only give and can never receive; in the other we can receive but never give. In the first attitude we propitiate others and call it a virtue, for they are giants and we are very small; in the second we dominate others and find some reasonable excuse for doing so, for we are bigger than they are, and they will be wise to recognise our superiority. The one is a false humility, the other a false pride. Pressed to its extreme limit, the one would lead to suicide, the other to insanity. But as true 'feeling' is restored, we can give, receive, and mutually share. We can then act as occasion requires and not as our needs dictate.

As we grow more used to the fact that some things will certainly go wrong (without it necessarily being our fault), that certain people will dislike us (because they are made that way), that our viewpoint will grow and develop (for judgments that we have made in the past will no longer seem so true in the future), 'acceptance' becomes a positive attitude to life. Like healthy children who accept the challenge of something more difficult to do, we can measure up to the problems which face us with zest and interest. Fear of failure need no longer haunt us, for failure falls into its proper place, not as an insuperable disaster, but as a pointer to the true solution. Being at ease of body and mind, we succeed in tackling problems of greater complexity, with less expenditure of energy than we wasted previously on objects of smaller importance. In the sense in which the engineer uses the word, we are growing more 'efficient' spiritually.

As the emphasis that has previously been placed on fighting and winning falls into the background, our health improves in every way. Our willpower can be conserved and used as a reserve to throw into the battle when the battle is really on; much less strain therefore is thrown for the rest of the time on the body's mechanism of attack and defence, and in particular on the suprarenal glands. These in their turn no longer need to drain the body of its resources, and the physical symptoms of disease begin to lose their origin and cause.

Positive acceptance (the true meaning of 'resist not evil) means that the primary attitude to life becomes analogous to the idea of eating and drinking. As a result of this plunge into a new way of living, 'feeling' comes into its own, and experience becomes 'suffering' in the proper meaning of the word. We take in, in order to give out. As our capacity for this increases, the risk of disease grows less, and if this way of life were more generally followed, disease would not be the disaster which it now seems. The emotional causes of ill-health are all the time being undermined and removed. As we grow closer to what St Theresa called the 'centre' of the Interior Castle, we lose our self-seeking attitudes and the need to defend them. Life becomes prayer, and prayer becomes life, for both are a taking in and giving out of energy. As we learn to follow St Paul's advice in Phil 9:6-7, we can give to God all the experiences of the day. As we turn all our thoughts and feelings into prayer, we are giving them to God outside us, and the more we do that, the more it seems that we can receive inwardly, as God is giving to us 'beyond measure'. As we feel more deeply, we become conscious of a Centre of our being (in the depths of the mind or the middle of the body) which is the source of Love and Life, the Indwelling Spirit, in which we learn to abide. St John of the Cross called it the Centre; the Eastern Church calls it the 'heart', and the 'prayer of the heart' (in the Philocalia) is the spiritual technique for abiding in the Centre. To this Christ was referring when He told the woman of Samaria that if she believed Him she need never thirst; for she would have (within her being) a well of living water springing up into eternal (or spiritual) life (John 4:14, 7:38). 'Feeling' within us is a stream of life which we give out and on which we continually draw. This Life was in Christ, the source of His power to heal, and those who have cleared their minds to some extent of the debris of anxiety, hostility and self-centredness, and so cleared the channel of life, in fact possess a power to heal. It is even more a capacity for 'sharing', in which we can come together in the unseen Presence of Christ, and share in His Love and His Life, His Body and His Blood, as 'branches of the Vine'. 'Feeling', which we now see to be essentially the Love of God, the very nature of reality, can then flood mind and body from within. This is not an emotional experience, for it occurs at a deeper level than that, but an experience of 'living in Spirit', that brings with it a deep peace and a lasting joy.

There is one thread, one law running through the universe: the taking in and giving out of energy. The body is doing it continually both eating and breathing to maintain life. The physical world of 'matter' is doing it continually, though we did not know that until the present century. In man it becomes a more conscious process in which he begins to have some power of choice. In his mind the process is first connected historically with the fact of breathing, so in ancient languages the word for breath (in Latin 'Spiritus') comes to denote the spiritual fact as well as the physical. 'The fruit of the Spirit is love, joy, peace, patience' (or suffering), and the other spiritual virtues, and healing as well. Mind and heart are at one, and heart supplies meaning where mind gives knowledge. 'He that abideth in love, abideth in God, and God in him.' In and through the world of matter, in and through our bodies, is that underlying reality of Spirit, in Whom 'we live and move and have our being'.

The prayer of faith

All healing comes from God who has given the doctor his knowledge and the nurse her skill. He guides and uses them all the more when they regard their work as His work and their gifts as gifts of the Spirit. Christianity is not opposed to medicine in any way and seeks only to inspire it. It would be foolish not to use any medical treatment that is likely to prove helpful; the only test to be applied is the simple one: am I relying on the medicine as medicine, or on God to work in me through the medicine? The doctor can be relied upon to withdraw the medicine when it is no longer of use; most doctors are weary of prescribing for patients unnecessarily. Do not forget that there is a spiritual victory to be won, and in that problem medical treatment can assist but cannot cure.

If you have called in the doctor, you have presumably decided that your sickness is not the will of God, and besides calling in the doctor, you should also 'call in the elders of the Church'. (Ideally the spiritually-minded doctor would be an elder of the Church.) Call them in, so that they know you are committed to seeking the spiritual answer to your problem. You may well need to open your heart to 'some discreet and learned minister of God's word', and to seek the ministry of understanding and forgiveness. Some will find help in confession to a priest, others in spiritual acknowledgment in God's presence alone. Whatever the means, there must be a sharing with God of whatever burden or difficulty may be oppressing one's life. Faith is not a straining of the will, but a state of spiritual rest and quiet expectation. It will be well, then, to learn how to rest, an art which we have largely forgotten, and the practice of 'relaxation' is now almost essential to health. By relaxing we begin to discover that deeper source of life within us, and relaxation becomes in effect a modern variant of the old technique of the 'prayer of the heart'.

We need to feed upon God continually in our inner life, so that we do not feel that a greater part of our waking life is lived apart from Him. That can be achieved most easily by the practice of turning our thoughts into prayers. In prayer we can pass through the mind everything that we have to do during the day, so that the thought of God's presence becomes the background of all our thinking and doing, and we do not feel that the world is taking us away from Him or He from us. As the burden of needless anxiety is lifted, so the flow of life is renewed.

As 'feeling' returns, faith becomes free; it is after all, as the writer to the Hebrews pointed out (11:1), 'putting our full confidence in things we hope for, being certain of things we cannot see' as Phillips translates it. 'Whatever you ask for in prayer, believe that you (always) receive them, and you shall have them.' Believing Christ's words, we shall pray and look for the answer. And the answer always comes. We may miss the answer, because it may not be the answer we expect, but the answer is always there, and as experience grows, we come to see more easily what the answer is. It will never be an escape from our troubles. Healing, or indeed God's answer to anything, always comes *through* the trouble. It may well be, for example, that the difficulty, physical or otherwise, has something to teach us that we have not yet learned. As we learn it, we shall find our way through, and come out safely on the other side. The more completely we can give ourselves to abiding, resting, trusting in God, the more complete the answer will be; and we need to thank God every day that His answer is coming to us.

We shall be drawn to pray too for the needs of others; the sick who pray for one another are richly rewarded in doing so, especially at the gathering together of the Church for 'the breaking of bread and prayer'. Can we pray for the sick who have been ill for a long time?

Will they be disappointed if our prayers are not answered? They will only be disappointed if they think of faith as an emotional heightening of tension. That is to be avoided in any case. If prayer helps them to bear their sickness, that is spiritual gain; if it keeps the disease in check (as it often does), that is gain too; if it gives them a compensating vision of spiritual truth (as it does to so many), that is a 'pearl of great price'. If it encourages them to find in their disease a spiritual lesson, and to probe the cause of their illness till they find out what is really the matter so that the disease has no further hold over them, that is best of all.

Very often the disease in itself is far less destructive than the repression which caused it and the fear that surrounds it. Many who have found help in chronic ill-health are most eager to extend that help to others, even where one might have expected them to be disappointed themselves.

Should we pray for the dying? It is always right to pray for people, but particularly so when they are dying or are being born! Prayer will help the new life into this world, and will help the old life into the new world. Death is not a tragedy, but a 'glorification', in which we pass from the small ante-chamber of life into a larger room, a new and glorious existence for which we are being made ready here. Christ assures us: 'in my Father's house are many mansions; if it were not so, I would have told you'. There is no reason why death, which is a natural process, should occur with pain, and we have a spiritual duty to help all souls from this life into the next, and we do so with greater thankfulness if they are discarding a physical 'envelope' which has been a heavy handicap to them. There is nothing morbid in prayer for the departing; if there is, it is our attitude that is at fault.

All prayer, in effect, follows the pattern of Christ's own prayer. We can start by repeating three times the cry of blind Bartimaeus by the wayside at Jericho (Mark 10:46), that Christ will hear us and come to our help. This reminds us that the Spirit of Christ is within us, and within all those with whom we are praying. Indeed, as the writer to the Hebrews reminds us, He is 'always spiritually intervening on our behalf' (Heb 7:25). We recognise and recollect the Name (or Presence) of the Father, as the unseen spiritual reality in whom we abide. We pray that all the sick may 'hallow' (recognise and enter into) the presence in this way, so that God's spiritual kingdom of fellowship and peace may be built up (and especially that the divisions in His Church may be healed). We pray that His will may be completely fulfilled in us, as His wisdom sees best for our lives, making use of all our desires for His glory and overruling them for good.

We pray for, and accept every day, everything necessary for the spiritual needs of our souls and the physical needs of our bodies. We forgive, and try to understand, the trespasses of others, that we may receive forgiveness of our own; and we pray that we may be brought through all difficulties that may face us, so that we gain spiritually and do not lose. In the end, we shall be so 'rooted and grounded in love' that we shall find spiritual maturity and physical well-being. Our house of faith will be built upon rock and not upon sand, and we shall be 'fellow-workers with God'.

Reverend Geoffrey Harding
1910-1994

Geoffrey Harding was a wartime chaplain in the R.A.F. who landed on Omaha Beach on D-Day and was awarded the M.C. He read philosophy and theology at Oxford University and worked as a parish priest with special interest in the ministry of healing. After the war he spent fifteen years with the Churches' Council of Healing, and was a founder member of the Institute of Religion and Medicine, an association of doctors and clergy. As a focal point for his belief that health, mental and spiritual, should and would follow reduction of stress, he founded the Relaxation Society which was set up in 1974 to publish literature, give lectures, and hold relaxation and meditation meetings. His views, formed during the early twentieth century, are now universally acknowledged.

In 1974 he was invited to take charge of the Church of St Mary Woolnoth, Lombard Street in the City of London, a centre for tackling stress. Within the Church, he pioneered the practice of relaxation and meditation, holding regular lunchtime relaxation meetings for city workers. The Society flourished during his lifetime and continues its good work in this field although his aura and charisma are much missed.